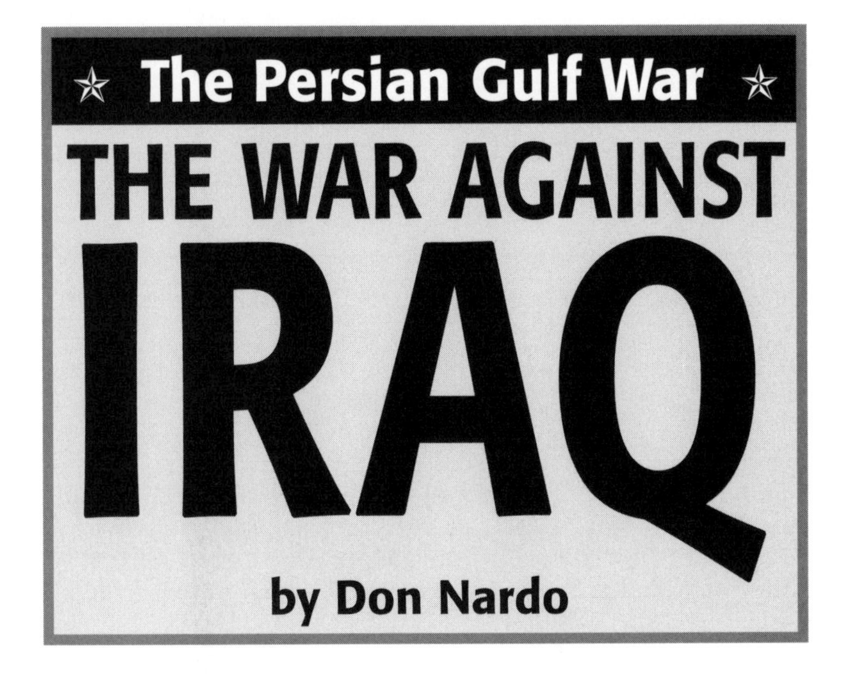

Lucent Books, P.O. Box 289011, San Diego, CA 92198-9011

Titles in The American War Library series include:

World War II
Hitler and the Nazis
Kamikazes
Leaders and Generals
Life as a POW
Life of an American Soldier in Europe
Strategic Battles in Europe
Strategic Battles in the Pacific
The War at Home
Weapons of War

The Civil War
Leaders of the North and South
Life Among the Soldiers and Cavalry
Lincoln and the Abolition of Slavery
Strategic Battles
Weapons of War

The Persian Gulf War
Leaders and Generals
Life of an American Soldier
The War Against Iraq
Weapons of War

The Vietnam War
A History of U.S. Involvement
The Home Front: Americans Protest the War
Leaders and Generals
Life of an American Soldier
Life as a POW
Weapons of War

Library of Congress Cataloging-in-Publication Data

Nardo, Don, 1947–
The war against Iraq / by Don Nardo.
p. cm.—(American war library: Persian Gulf)
Includes bibliographical references and index.
Summary: Discusses the Persian Gulf War including the Iraqi invasion of Kuwait, "Desert Shield," the ominous prelude to all-out war, "Desert Storm," the massive Allied air assault, the lightning Allied ground offensive, and the continuing troubles for Iraq and the Middle East.
ISBN 1-56006-715-2 (alk. paper)
1. Persian Gulf War, 1991—Juvenile literature.
[1. Persian Gulf War, 1991.] I. Title.
DS79.723 N37 2001
956.7044'2—dc21 00-009318

P.O. Box 289011, San Diego, California 92198-9011

Printed in the U.S.A.

19.95

☆ Contents ☆

★ Foreword ★

A Nation Forged by War

The United States, like many nations, was forged and defined by war. Despite Benjamin Franklin's opinion that "There never was a good war or a bad peace," the United States owes its very existence to the War of Independence, one to which Franklin wholeheartedly subscribed. The country forged by war in 1776 was tempered and made stronger by the Civil War in the 1860s.

The Texas Revolution, the Mexican-American War, and the Spanish-American War expanded the country's borders and gave it overseas possessions. These wars made the United States a world power, but this status came with a price, as the nation became a key but reluctant player in both World War I and World War II.

Each successive war further defined the country's role on the world stage. Following World War II, U.S. foreign policy redefined itself to focus on the role of defender, not only of the freedom of its own citizens, but also of the freedom of people everywhere. During the cold war that followed World War II until the collapse of the Soviet Union, defending the world meant fighting communism. This goal, manifested in the Korean and Vietnam conflicts, proved elusive, and soured the American public on its achievability. As the United States emerged as the world's sole superpower, American foreign policy has been guided less by national interest and more on protecting international human rights. But as involvement in Somalia and Kosovo prove, this goal has been equally elusive.

As a result, the country's view of itself changed. Bolstered by victories in World Wars I and II, Americans first relished the role of protector. But, as war followed war in a seemingly endless procession, Americans began to doubt their leaders, their motives, and themselves. The Vietnam War especially caused people to question the validity of sending its young people to die in places where they were not particularly wanted and for people who did not seem especially grateful.

While the most obvious changes brought about by America's wars have been geopolitical in nature, many other aspects of society have been touched. War often does not bring about change directly, but acts instead like the catalyst in a chemical reaction, accelerating changes already in progress.

Some of these changes have been societal. The role of women in the United States had been slowly changing, but World War II put thousands into the workforce and into uniform. They might have gone back to being housewives after the war, but equality, once experienced, would not be forgotten.

Likewise, wars have accelerated technological change. The necessity for faster airplanes and a more destructive bomb led to the development of jet planes and nuclear energy. Artificial fibers developed for parachutes in the 1940s were used in the clothing of the 1950s.

Lucent Books' American War Library covers key wars in the development of the nation. Each war is covered in several volumes, to allow for more detail, context, and to provide volumes on often neglected subjects, such as the kamikazes of World War II, or weapons used in the Civil War. As with all Lucent Books, notes, annotated bibliographies, and appendixes such as glossaries give students a launching point for further research. In addition, sidebars and archival photographs enhance the text. Together, each volume in The American War Library will aid students in understanding how America's wars have shaped and changed its politics, economics, and society.

☆ Introduction ☆

A Short but Significant Conflict

People around the world were stunned on August 2, 1990, by alarming news. The Middle Eastern country of Iraq, led by its president, Saddam Hussein (commonly called Saddam for short), had suddenly invaded Kuwait, its much smaller neighbor. In only three days, more than 100,000 Iraqi troops took control of Kuwait's capital, Kuwait City, seized the country's rich oil fields, and forced the Kuwaiti royal family into exile.

For months, heads of state and diplomats from many countries around the globe tried to persuade Saddam to remove his troops. His continued refusals finally convinced the United States and the United Nations to use military force against Iraq. The war that ensued was short but decisive. Beginning on January 16, 1991, U.S. and other U.N.-sponsored forces destroyed Iraq's industrial and war-making facilities, crushed most of the Iraqi army, and liberated Kuwait, all in just forty-three days.

Though the war was relatively brief in duration, as wars go, its effects on the United States, the Middle East, and the global community were significant. In the U.S., success in the Gulf War sparked renewed feelings of pride and confidence among Americans. Before the war began, many in the U.S. had worried that the country might become involved in another long, costly, and unpopular war like the Vietnam conflict of the 1960s and 1970s. Addressing these worries shortly before the outbreak of fighting, President George Bush said, "In our country, I know that there are fears of another Vietnam. Let me assure you, should military action be required, this will not be another Vietnam. This will not be another protracted, drawn-out war."[1] In fact, by the war's successful conclusion, worries of another Vietnam had ended, as one U.S. army commander declared proudly, "The stigma of Vietnam has been erased."[2]

The Gulf War was also significant for the people of the Middle East. For decades, most of the tension and fighting in the region had been between the Arab countries and Israel. Most Arabs were united in their hatred for Israel and their distrust of foreign powers that backed the Israelis, including the United States. Saddam Hussein's takeover of Kuwait and subsequent defeat marked the first instance ever in which Middle Eastern nations joined foreigners to fight another Middle Eastern nation.

In addition, the Gulf War involved still another important first. Never before in its forty-five-year history had the United Nations taken such a tough political and military stand against a country's naked aggression. Many people felt that the United Nations was at last fulfilling the function for which it had been created—to ensure that the nations of the world live in peace. "Many small countries could well see the implications for their own security if predators" such as Saddam Hussein "were allowed to prosper," remarks King's College scholar Lawrence Freedman.

A Kuwaiti girl proudly waves her country's flag shortly after the liberation of Kuwait City.

> The respect of the sovereignty of states and the sanctity of national borders has long been a central principle of international order. The idea that it should be enforced by the international community as a whole can be traced back to President Woodrow Wilson's concept of collective security on which the League of Nations, and later the United Nations, were predicated [established]. The main difference between the Gulf conflict and previous instances of collective action (such as Korea [i.e., the Korean War in the early 1950s]) lay in the unprecedented ability [of the United Nations] to respond to such a blatant challenge and to carry the response through to its logical conclusion.[3]

The U.N.'s strong response to Iraq's invasion of Kuwait certainly did not constitute any sort of guarantee that there will be no similar aggressions in the future. But the international organization had sent a clear signal to all countries that, in the years to come, the world community will not likely stand by and tolerate such aggressions.

Chapter 1

Middle Eastern Sands Sow the Seeds of Crisis

For more than forty centuries, the Middle East has been one of the most crucial, controversial, and fought over areas in the world. One reason for this is the region's strategic location. Because it lies at the crossroads of three continents—Europe, Asia, and Africa—people who lived in these continents had to pass through the Middle East to establish trade and military routes, and to protect these routes, various nations and peoples, inside and outside of the region, attacked, conquered, and/or tried to control it.

Struggles over Land and Self-Rule

Throughout most of the modern era, until the early to mid–twentieth century, foreign powers controlled the Middle East, and the native peoples of the area had little or no control over the land. A great many of the natives were and remain Arabs, peoples originally descended from ancient Semitic tribes. Even as late as the opening of the twentieth century, the Arabs belonged to numerous small tribes scattered across the Middle East, most of them living in tents and making their livings by herding, trading, or fishing. These tribes often fought one another over land, water, and countless other issues. At the time, the Ottoman Turks, who ruled a large empire centered in Turkey (lying south of the Black Sea), controlled much of the Middle East. Even though Arabs were generally unhappy with Turkish rule, they could only dream of driving out the Turks, who were, in comparison, militarily very organized and powerful. The reality was that, as long as the Arabic tribes remained divided, the Turks easily maintained their control of the region.

This situation changed dramatically during World War I, however. During that momentous global conflict, the British, French, Americans, and their allies fought against the Germans and their allies, who included the Turks. The British and French wanted to force the Turks of the Middle East

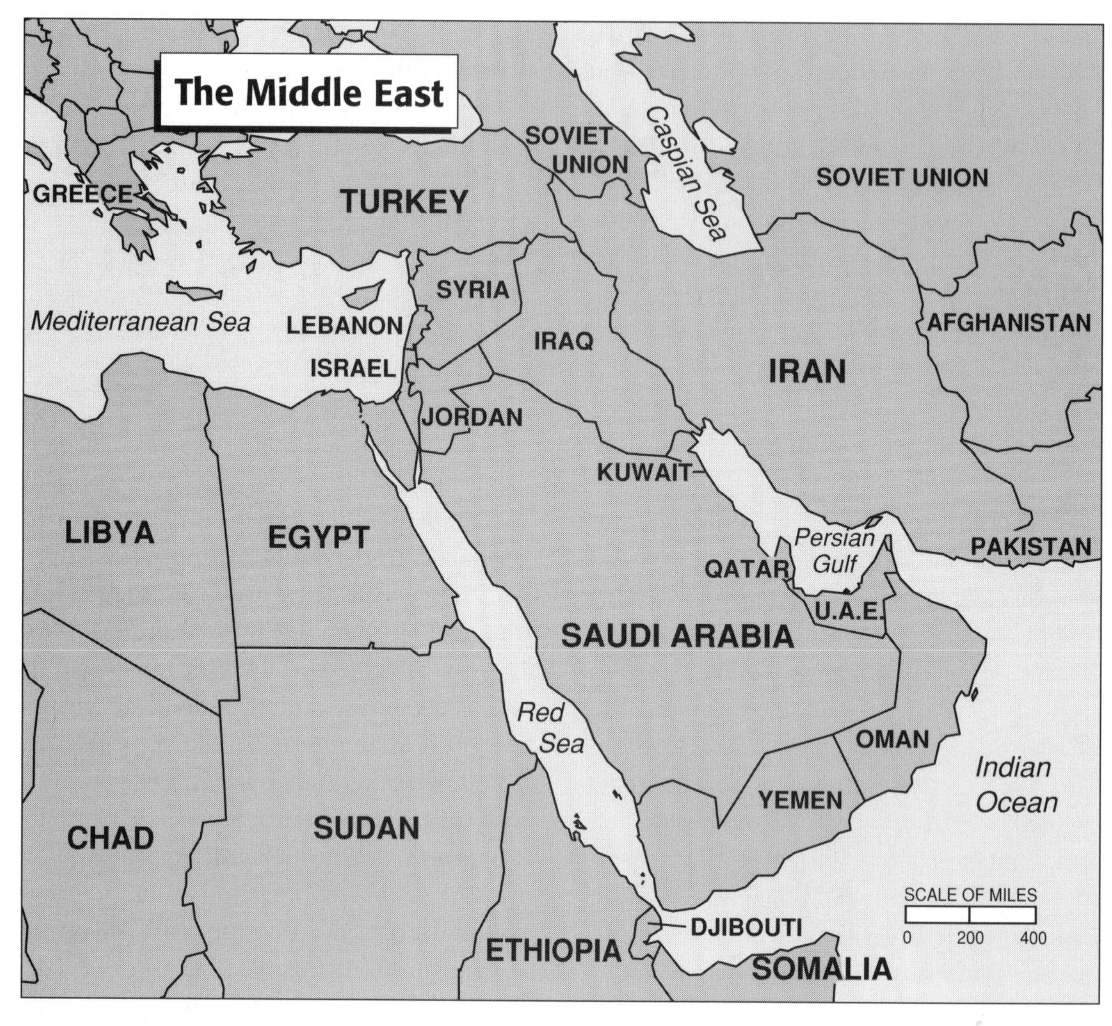

to reduce the size of and weaken the Ottoman Empire. They also wanted to control the Middle East after the war, for both the strategic and material advantages the region offered. In 1916, the British succeeded in briefly uniting a number of the Arab tribes and organizing them in a revolt against the Turks. This marked the first time in centuries that the tribes had achieved any kind of unity. British leaders were successful because they promised the Arabs that if they helped to defeat the Turks, Britain would allow them to establish their own nations in the area.

Aided by the Arabs, the British, French, and their allies were able to drive the Turks out of the Middle East. Consequently, Britain and France, then the two most powerful European nations, controlled the area at the close of World War I. The Arabs expected to receive their promised reward—the right to set up their own countries—but Britain and France did not keep their end of the bargain. Instead, the Europeans divided most of the western reaches of the Middle East into separate territories and administered them under their own mandates (authority to govern). In the process, they assured Arab leaders that various parts of the region would be granted independence in the future, when the British and French believed the time was right.

An Arab soldier sits atop his camel during World War I. A number of Arab tribes achieved temporary unity during this conflict, thanks to British efforts.

The Arabs naturally protested, and in some cases actually attempted to set up their own governments, but these efforts were in vain. A typical example was the situation in the region that would later become Iraq. In 1920, at a meeting in the city of Baghdad, writes Dilip Hiro, an expert on Middle Eastern affairs,

> a group dominated by nationalist Iraqi military officers who had opposed Ottoman suzerainty [domination] in the past, declared Iraq to be independent under the constitutional reign of Abdullah ibn Hussein, a younger brother of Faisal I ibn Hussein [who at the same time declared himself the ruler of an independent Syria]. These declarations of independence were rejected by Britain and France. In July 1920 the French defeated the forces of King Faisal I, and imposed their mandate. Faisal I then accepted the throne of Iraq offered to him by Abdullah. . . . Britain spent the better part of the summer and autumn of 1920 crushing the popular [Arab] movement against its military rule in Iraq.[4]

Though the Arabs had achieved temporary unity, at the time they lacked the wealth and military power needed to stand up to the Europeans. And this setback created a great deal of Arab resentment against all European nations, especially Britain and France.

This resentment remained strong in the years that followed. This was mainly because Britain and France, who had exploited their status as world-class powers to impose their mandates on the peoples of the Middle East, had those mandates approved by the League of Nations. (This international organization, set up at the end of World War I, was the precursor of the United Nations.) Bending to political pressure from Britain, France, and their allies, the league essentially gave the British and French permission to develop the Middle Eastern territories in any manner they saw fit until they felt comfortable in granting them independence. Britain retained control of Iraq, Jordan, and Palestine (the coastal region that now comprises Israel), while France continued to administer Syria, which included what would later become the nation of Lebanon.

Still, the Europeans recognized that they could not effectively control and exploit the Arabs and their territories without the aid of popular Arab leaders. The British and French accordingly sought the cooperation of such local leaders, and, among other things, this set in motion the chain of events leading to the elevation of Iraq's status from a territory, to a dependent national state, and finally to an independent country recognized by the international community. "In March 1921," Hiro explains,

> London opted for indirect rule of Iraq through a local government with an Arab leader. Finding Faisal I suitable for the position, the British installed him as king in August. To formalize relations with Iraq, Britain incorporated the terms of its League of Nations mandate into a treaty. . . . The Anglo-Iraqi Treaty of 1922, which vested economic and military control of Iraq in British hands, was then placed before [a local Iraqi] assembly elected in March 1924. The reluctant members ratified it only after the British high commissioner had threatened to suspend the constitution. . . . [British] interest in Iraq was heightened by the discovery [in 1927] of oil in Mosul [a province of northern Iraq]. Aware of the economic benefits of petroleum, the Iraqi government improved its relations with London. It was against this background that in September 1929 Britain agreed in principle to sponsor Iraq's membership in the League of Nations.[5]

In October 1932, the British ended their mandate over Iraq, which was now, at least on paper, a full-fledged country. However, for Britain's help in gaining that status, the Iraqis had to sign a twenty-five-year treaty granting the British the right to station their forces in the country. Independent or not, the emerging nations of the Middle East were clearly still tied to Europe's apron strings.

The Zionist Factor

Arab resentment against European meddling in the Middle East also centered around another issue in which Britain was heavily involved. This was the British desire to set up a Jewish homeland in Palestine. During World War I, to get Jewish support for their war effort, the British began making promises to a group of European Jews known as Zionists. The Zionists advocated that Jews living around the world should be allowed to administer their own nation in the Palestinian lands that their ancestors had occupied in biblical times. Popular scholar Max Dimont explains how the British involvement with the Zionists first developed:

> England's brilliant chemist, Chaim Weizmann [who was Jewish], had been called into the British War Office to find a way of producing synthetic cordite, an explosive essential to the British War effort. . . . Weizmann discovered such a process and turned it over to the British government. When, therefore, in 1917, Weizmann, an ardent Zionist, an eloquent speaker, and a man of great personal magnetism, approached the British government with a request that it assume a protectorate for a national Jewish home in Palestine, he received a favorable reply. Through Lord Balfour, the British Foreign Secretary, the British government let it be known (November 2, 1917) that "His Majesty's Government views with favor the establishment in Palestine of a national home for the Jewish people." Jubilation among the Jews was great.[6]

The Origins of Zionism

Palestine was the ancient home of the Jewish people. And it was there that the original state of Israel, the kingdom of David and Solomon, thrived some three thousand years ago. Over the course of the centuries, most Jews were scattered around the world, a phenomenon called the Diaspora. But the desire to return to Zion (the holy city of Jerusalem and its Palestinian environs) long remained an important part of Jewish tradition. In 1882, a small group of Jews adopted the name "Lovers of Zion" and founded a community in Palestine. They hoped that other Jews from around the world would follow their lead and return to the land of their ancestors. A few years later, Theodor Herzl, an Austrian journalist, published *The Jewish State,* in which he pointed out that Jews were considered outsiders in every nation and continually suffered persecution. Only by forming their own nation, he said, could they live in complete freedom and dignity. In 1897, Herzl organized the first Zionist congress in Switzerland. The official goal of the organization was to create for the Jewish people a homeland in Palestine secured by public law. During World War I, the British endorsed the Zionists. And in 1917, a British leader issued the now famous Balfour Declaration, committing Britain to helping the Jews find a homeland.

Lord Balfour's statement on the matter became known as the Balfour Declaration. When the League of Nations approved the British mandate for Palestine in 1922, it also approved the Balfour Declaration, and many Western nations, including the United States, publicly supported the idea of a Jewish state in Palestine. These countries had large, influential local Jewish communities that pressured their governments to support the Zionists. In response to the declaration, Jews from many parts of the world began emigrating to the Middle East, believing that the British would eventually grant them an independent nation.

Not surprisingly, the Arabs strongly opposed this idea of establishing a Jewish state in their midst. They believed that, since most people living in the area were Arabs, Palestine was an Arab land. They held that it mattered little who had occupied the region in ancient times and that those who inhabited it in modern times had a stronger claim to ownership. The Arabs also felt that it was unfair for the Western countries to impede the establishment of independent Arab nations and at the same time to create an independent Jewish state in the Middle East. Most Arab leaders interpreted British support for a Jewish homeland as an attempt to gain a Western power base in the region. A Jewish state, with its strings being pulled by British leaders in London, would allow Britain to maintain its influence in the area even after the Arabs had managed to gain their independence. Arab bitterness over Britain's pro-Zionist policies marked the beginning of the Arab-Jewish conflict that remains unresolved to this day in the Middle East.

The Quest for Buried Riches

The Arabs were also bitter over Western exploitation of the natural resources of the Middle East. Clearly, both Britain and France strongly coveted local oil reserves, as evidenced by the deal struck with the Iraqis in the early 1930s; by insisting on the right to keep troops stationed in Iraq, the British ensured that they would maintain their influence in the country, including access to its rich oil fields. The Arabs in Iraq and other parts of the Middle East believed that the oil belonged to them, but they admittedly lacked the money and expertise to extract and refine the oil. In fact, oil became one of the primary reasons for fighting in the region, both between Arabs and Westerners and among the Arabs themselves; the quest for oil was certainly one of the major motivations behind Iraq's invasion of Kuwait in 1990.

One major aspect of the oil issue was that in the 1920s large Western nations such as Britain and the United States became dependent on Middle Eastern oil. Before World War I, the British produced less than 5 percent of the world's oil. However, when they took control of Iraq after the war, they gained some of the Middle East's largest oil fields and, by 1919, Britain was producing more than half of the world's oil. The U.S. vigorously protested Britain's attempt to corner the world oil market. U.S. leaders argued that they had supplied Britain with oil during the great war and therefore deserved a fair share of the valuable oil supplies from the Middle East. After continued protests and negotiations, the British allowed five U.S. companies to operate in Iraq in 1928. And in the following years, U.S. oil corporations expanded their operations into other Middle

Islam: The Faith of the Arabs

Differences in religion have been a major source of tension and misunderstanding among Arabs, Israelis, and Westerners over the centuries and contributed to the tensions of the Gulf War. While the Jews ascribe to Judaism and most Westerners are Christians, the Arabs practice Islam, which helps to shape their laws, family and social customs, and worldviews. Practiced by more than 800 million people worldwide, Islam is the world's second largest religion after Christianity. Followers of Islam, called Muslims, adhere to the teachings of the prophet Muhammad, who was born about A.D. 570 in Mecca, an Arabian town near the coast of the Red Sea. According to Muslim tradition, Muhammad received a series of messages from God (whom the Muslims refer to as Allah), and the contents of these revelations became the basis for Islam's holiest book, the Koran.

Muhammad began teaching the principles of Islam, which include recognizing Allah as the one true God, submitting fully to God's will, and following strict moral rules. And the faith quickly began gaining converts. Fearing that the prophet might become too powerful and upset the established order, local rulers started persecuting Muslims, forcing Muhammad and seventy of his followers to flee, in 622, to Medina, about two hundred miles north of Mecca. Muslims mark this flight, called the Hegira, as the beginning of the Islamic calendar.

Muhammad soon succeeded in converting the population of Medina to Islam, and in 630 he led a small army in the conquest of Mecca. He forced the local residents to convert, and Mecca and Medina became the holy cities of the faith. Thereafter, Muhammad advocated the concept of "jihad," then meaning "spiritual struggle," to spread the faith to nonbelievers. After his death in 632, many of his followers interpreted jihad to mean "holy war," and in the following years Muslim armies conquered all the peoples of the Arabian peninsula. They then spread outward, and by 717 the Muslims controlled large portions of India, central Asia, northern Africa, and southern Spain.

Islam is partly based on the teachings and ideas of Judaism and Christianity. For instance, Muslims view large portions of the Old and New Testaments as holy books and recognize a long line of Judeo-Christian prophets, including Abraham, Moses, and Jesus. Muslims believe that a rejection of Islam is the same as rejection of God and is, therefore, the main cause of chaos and confusion in the world. According to the rules of the faith, Muslims must be charitable to the poor and pray five times a day while facing in the direction of Mecca. They must also make a pilgrimage to that city at least once during their lives.

While praying, two Muslim men bow toward the holy city of Mecca. This Arabian site was the birthplace of Islam's chief prophet, Muhammad.

Eastern areas, including Kuwait (which even then Iraqi leaders claimed should be part of Iraq). By 1938, the U.S. controlled more of the region's oil reserves than any other nation, and Americans increasingly relied on Middle Eastern oil. The need to protect these oil interests became an important reason for later U.S. intervention in Middle Eastern affairs, including the Gulf War against Iraq.

During the 1920s and 1930s, the Arabs felt compelled to cooperate with Western oil companies. This was because the Arabs badly needed the advanced technical knowledge and oil equipment imported by the British and Americans. This situation remained largely unchanged until another world war altered the balance of power in the Middle East.

American oil workers adjust their drilling equipment.

A New Arab Unity Emerges

During World War II, the old colonial empires of powerful European nations like France and Britain broke up. These countries found that they had done all they could do to fight the war and could no longer effectively maintain so many far-flung colonies. Therefore, many of these colonies around the world gained their independence, including some in the Middle East. France, for example, granted independence to Syria in 1941 and to Lebanon in 1943. By the closing months of the war in 1944, Britain was the only foreign power still occupying the Middle East, and more and more Arabs were demanding that the British withdraw once and for all.

It was in support of this demand that the Arabs once more gained a measure of unity, in this case a more lasting one. On March 22, 1945, representatives from the seven existing independent Middle Eastern states met in Cairo, the capital of Egypt. Iraq, Egypt, Trans-Jordan, Yemen, Saudi Arabia, Syria, and Lebanon established the Arab League, with the goal of working for the common interests of all Arabs. But personal rivalries and other differences among several of the member states prevented the new organization from reaching initial agreements.

There was one topic, however, on which all seven members of the Arab League agreed, namely that they strongly opposed the creation of a Jewish homeland in Palestine. In fact, the establishment of a Jewish state became a major international issue directly following World War II. Millions of European Jews had been massacred by the German Nazi regime, and hundreds of thousands of displaced Jews suffered in refugee camps. Many countries, including the United States, pressured Britain to withdraw from Palestine to allow these Jews to set up their own independently run nation. In 1947, the British finally gave in to the pressure and announced that they would withdraw from Palestine on May 15, 1948.

Hearing this news, the United Nations, the world organization set up at the end of World War II, immediately began discussing what should be done about Palestine and the Jews. After numerous intense arguments and debates, the U.N. voted on November 29, 1947, to partition (divide) Palestine into two states after the British pullout. One state would be Jewish, the other Arab, and both would share the capital city of Jerusalem, to be administered by the U.N. The Jews were elated, but the Arabs, still solidly against the notion of a Jewish homeland in the region, completely rejected the U.N. plan. The Arab League called for Arabs all over the Middle East to prevent the plan from going into effect. And during the following months there were many skirmishes, ambushes, and acts of terrorism between Arab and Jewish guerrilla armies in Palestine.

Israel Is Born

On May 14, 1948, the day before the final British evacuation, an announcement from Palestine electrified the world. David Ben-Gurion, the leader of the Jewish forces, formally proclaimed the establishment of

David Ben Gurion, who led the Jewish forces in Palestine in the late 1940s and announced the formation of the state of Israel.

the nation of Israel. The Jews had decided to declare their independence before the U.N. had officially granted it. By doing this, they were able to postpone the U.N. decision to partition Palestine and acquired more direct control over the fate of their new nation. The United States immediately recognized the new state, as did the Soviet Union and most other members of the United Nations. But just as quickly, the members of the Arab League declared war on Israel, and soon armies from six Arab nations marched into Palestine.

Israeli soldiers inspect an Egyptian fighter plane that ditched in the sea after being shot down only six hours after the start of the 1948 Arab-Israeli war.

The resulting 1948 Arab-Israeli war lasted less than eight months. Even though the combined population of the Arab states was some forty times larger than that of Israel, the Israelis won a resounding victory. During the conflict, Israeli forces succeeded in capturing some of the lands the U.N. had designated to the Arabs, and by January 1949 Israel controlled 30 percent more territory than the U.N. had originally assigned it. Hundreds of thousands of Arabs who lived in the newly captured territories became refugees or had to live under Israeli authority. The problem of what to do about these displaced people, called the Palestinians, has been an obstacle to Middle Eastern peace ever since.

Angry and humiliated over their defeat, many Arabs criticized the United States for recognizing and supporting Israel during the 1948 war. Convinced that the U.S. would continue to back and strengthen Israel, several Arab nations turned to the Soviet Union for financial and military aid. The Soviets were more than happy to supply the Arabs with both money and weapons. At the same time, to counter Soviet influence in the region, as well as to help Israel, the U.S. became more aligned with the Israelis and increasingly involved in Middle Eastern affairs.

The United States developed a Middle Eastern policy that centered on four major goals. First, the U.S. dedicated itself to ensuring the security of Israel, which included supplying the nation with weapons and other military aid. Second, U.S. leaders vowed to work for an Arab-Israeli peace settlement. The third U.S. objective was to maintain American access to Middle Eastern oil, a vital commodity to the U.S. economy. And fourth, the U.S. sought to keep the Arabs from becoming too friendly with the Soviets, with whom the Americans were locked in the so-called cold war.

Arab leaders often criticized these U.S. goals as insincere and contradictory. For example, they accused the United States of caring more about Arab oil than about the Arabs themselves. In addition, the Arabs insisted that the U.S. could not hope to bring peace to the region until it stopped backing Israel. So Arab-American relations remained strained in the ensuing years, as more bloody conflicts continued to wrack the Middle East.

Arab Quarrels with Israel and the West Continue

Indeed, the Arabs increasingly refused to accept Israel's right to exist and searched for ways to weaken and disrupt the Jewish state. In 1956, Egypt boldly seized control of the Suez Canal, the vital shipping channel connecting the Mediterranean and Red Seas, which was owned by Britain, France, and other European nations and operated by Britain. The Egyptians refused to guarantee the safety of Israeli shipping, hoping to cut off supply lines to Israel. Israeli forces then retaliated by attacking Egypt on October 29 and quickly fought their way toward the canal. The surprised Egyptians soon found that they had to contend with more than just the Israelis. On November 5, British and French forces joined in the battle against the Egyptians, and by November 7 these allies had regained control of the canal.

Arabs and Israelis clashed again in 1967. Egypt moved troops toward the Israeli border and at the same time imposed a blockade on Israeli shipping. Meanwhile, other Arab countries began to mobilize their troops. Correctly reasoning that they were about to be invaded from all sides, the Israelis attacked Egypt, Jordan, and Syria on June 5. Israeli jets managed to destroy the Egyptian air force while it was still on the ground, and in just six days Israel crippled the Arab armies and captured borderlands belonging to Syria and Jordan.

During the next six years, tensions in the Middle East remained high as the

During the 1956 Suez crisis, a salvage ship attempts to clear the canal of two vessels sunk by the Egyptians to block the waterway.

United States built up the Israeli military and the Soviet Union continued to supply arms to the Arabs. Carrying the fight beyond Middle Eastern borders, Arab terrorists hijacked commercial airliners and attacked civilians in many parts of the world. Clearly, the Arabs were determined to get back the lands they had lost in the previous wars and to destroy Israel once and for all. And to this end, on October 6, 1973, Arab armies launched a surprise attack on Israel. At first, they gained some ground. But eventually the Israelis drove them back and once more defeated them.

U.S.-Arab relations became particularly strained during the 1973 Arab-Israeli conflict. The Organization of Petroleum Exporting Countries (OPEC), most of whose members were Arabs, wanted to pressure the United States into ceasing its support for Israel. So a majority of OPEC members voted to raise the price of oil to levels four times higher than normal. Then, OPEC cut off oil supplies to the U.S. and several other countries, an oil embargo that resulted in gas rationing and economic troubles for many Americans. The U.S. did not react by giving up its support for Israel, but it did work harder to negotiate settlements acceptable to both sides. Convinced that the U.S. would be more evenhanded in the future, the Arabs lifted the embargo in 1974.

Conflicts over Control of the Gulf

When the Arabs raised oil prices in the 1970s, some Middle Eastern countries grew quite wealthy. Iraq, Saudi Arabia, and Kuwait (which Britain had granted independence in 1961) benefited enormously from the growing oil profits. The quest for wealth also generated increased tensions among the oil-producing nations them-

Israeli heavy artillery blasts away during the 1973 Arab-Israeli conflict. The Arabs made some initial gains but were eventually defeated.

selves. For instance, both Iraq and its eastern neighbor Iran wanted to control oil shipping in the Persian Gulf, the 650-mile-long bay that borders both countries in the south. This rivalry reopened an old and bitter Iraqi-Iranian dispute.

Since the 1800s, the two peoples had argued and fought over the Shatt al Arab waterway, located on the northern edge of the Persian Gulf. Vital to trade, the waterway was essential to the economies of both nations. In 1979, the dispute intensified and each side threatened the other. Then, on September 17, 1980, Iraq's president, Saddam Hussein, claimed complete control of the Shatt al Arab and forbade ships flying the Iranian flag to enter. Five days later, Iraqi troops invaded Iran and destroyed key Iranian oil installations, after which the Iranians counterattacked, blowing up many Iraqi oil facilities.

The eight-year-long war that followed, today often referred to as the "First" Gulf War, was the bloodiest yet seen in the modern Middle East. An estimated 1 million people died in the conflict, as both sides launched missile attacks on cities and other civilian targets and used deadly chemical weapons on the battlefield. Regarding the latter devices, in March 1984 Iraq became the first nation in history to use toxic nerve gases on the battlefield, a move one Iraqi commander justified in the following cold-blooded manner: "If you gave me a pesticide to throw at these worms of insects [i.e., the Iranians] to make them breathe [it] and become exterminated, I'd use it."[7] Despite resorting to such extreme means, however, neither Iraq nor Iran emerged from the war as a clear winner. In fact, when the U.N. negotiated a cease-fire in 1988, both countries controlled approximately the same territory they had at the beginning of the war.

The Iraq-Iran war put a huge financial strain on Iraq. During the conflict, Iraq built up the largest military force in the Middle East, using much of its vast oil wealth to buy missiles, tanks, artillery, and other weapons from France, the Soviet Union, the United States, and other nations. Iraq received additional money for weapons and other war supplies from rich Arab neighbors, Saudi Arabia and Kuwait in particular. In all, Iraq spent hundreds of billions of dollars buying weapons, waging war, and rebuilding destroyed oil facilities. In 1990, the country was heavily in debt, and Saddam Hussein desperately needed money. He wanted to find a way to eliminate Iraq's debts, to expand the country's economy, and to gain control of the Persian Gulf. The strategy he chose to achieve these goals would soon plunge his people and the peoples of other Middle Eastern nations into yet another disastrous war.

☆ Chapter 2 ☆

The Iraqi Invasion of Kuwait

The 1990 invasion of Kuwait was part of a long effort by Saddam Hussein to expand Iraq's power, influence, wealth, and prestige. Ever since becoming leader of Iraq in 1979, Saddam had dreamed of restoring Iraq to its former greatness. His goal was to use money from the country's oil industry to transform Iraq into a modern version of Babylon, the ancient capital of the mighty Babylonian Empire that had once occupied the same region. Saddam even began rebuilding sections of Babylon's ruins to symbolize the power and glory of modern Iraq.

But it was his own image, not that of the Iraqi people, that Saddam sought most to enhance. The fact was that he wanted to increase his prestige with all Arabs and exercise a controlling influence over the course of Middle Eastern affairs. He came, rather arrogantly, to call himself the "Knight of the Arab Nation," supposedly the only leader strong and brave enough to unite all Arabs and to stand up to Israel and its Western supporters. And indeed, not a few Arabs began to look at him as their champion. Most Jordanians, for example, who were still bitter over their losses in the Arab-Israeli wars, strongly backed Saddam. In addition, a considerable number of Palestinian Arabs living in Israel praised him, believing that he supported their cause for a Palestinian homeland separate from Israel. For that reason, the Palestinian Liberation Organization (PLO), an Arab group fighting to establish such a homeland, also embraced Saddam with enthusiasm. None of these supporters expected him to invade a fellow Arab country, and that ended up hurting his image with many Arabs.

Saddam's Quest for Power and Prestige

During the 1980s, to maintain his authority in Iraq, Saddam did not hesitate to rule with an iron hand. According to the country's constitution, Iraq is a republic, a state

One of the many huge photos and paintings of Saddam erected throughout Iraq to honor him as "Knight of the Arab Nation."

with a national assembly run by representatives of the people. But after taking power, Saddam became a dictator, exercising total control over the government, the army, the press, and the oil industry. Anyone daring to speak out against him was summarily tortured and/or executed. And not surprisingly, many Iraqi politicians, writers, and businesspeople fled to other countries to escape Saddam's tyranny. In the meantime, he made sure that most of the money the country made from oil was used to support the military or ended up in his own bank accounts. So most of the Iraqi people—merchants, farmers, herders, and laborers alike—remained poor.

As a way to extend his power and prestige beyond Iraq's borders, Saddam waged an eight-year campaign against Iran. He wanted to expand Iraq's and his own wealth by eliminating Iran as a competitor in the lucrative Persian Gulf oil industry. He also sought to bolster his image with Arab nations who disliked Iran. Many Arabs, including the Kuwaitis and Saudis, looked on the non-Arabic Iranians as a potential economic and military threat, and Saddam correctly reasoned that fighting the Iranians would increase his popularity in

Two Iranian soldiers prepare for battle during the bloody Iraq-Iran War, which raged from 1980 to 1988.

Iraq's Turbulent but Proud Past

Modern Iraqis often proudly point out that their land was one of the first places where human civilization grew and prospered. Indeed, historians believe that the fertile valleys of the region's Tigris and Euphrates Rivers supported widespread agriculture and organized communities over seven thousand years ago. There, the ancient Sumerian civilization grew and flourished, building cities, making pottery, smelting metals, and recording its language in writing. The area became known as Mesopotamia, meaning "the land between the rivers." Eventually the Babylonian Empire rose in the region and extended its control over much of the Middle East. Babylon, one of the greatest cities of the ancient world, was the home of the lush Hanging Gardens, one of the seven wonders of the ancient world. In time, however, the Babylonian realm weakened and fell and a succession of foreign conquerors, including Persians, Greeks, and Romans, occupied Iraq.

It was in the seventh century A.D. that Iraq came under the control of the fast-growing Arab empire established by the followers of the prophet Muhammad; at that time the people of the area converted to Islam, which remains the nation's principal religion. Under the rule of the Arabs, Baghdad, Iraq's capital, became a wealthy and renowned center of learning, culture, science, and the arts. But the thirteenth-century invasion by the Mongols, a nomadic Asiatic people, caused the area to decline rapidly, and during centuries of Mongol and later Turkish domination, most Iraqis were poor and illiterate. When Turkish rule ended during World War I, the British administered Iraq, and even though they granted the country independence in 1932, they continued to exert a strong influence over its affairs until the late 1950s.

After several bloody power struggles between rival Iraqi political factions in the 1960s, the Ba'ath party took control of Iraq. The Ba'athists are strongly pan-Arab, believing that all Arabs should unite against Israel and the Western nations. Ba'athist leaders sought to control all aspects of Iraqi society, and Saddam Hussein, who came to power in 1979, was no exception. He suppressed ethnic and language differences and tried to make his citizens adhere to Ba'athist beliefs and ideas, often using the army and his own secret police to enforce his will on the people.

A modern depiction of the Hanging Gardens of Babylon, one of the Seven Wonders of the Ancient World.

the Arab world. Indeed, his struggle with Iran, coupled with his staunch anti-Israeli policies, made him appear a hero in the eyes of a good many Arabs, particularly the Jordanians and Palestinians.

Saddam also sought the support of Western countries that opposed the Iranians. Because Iran's government was fanatically against any Western influences in the Middle East, the United States and other Western nations supported Iraq in its struggle against Iran. Hoping that Saddam would defeat the Iranians, the U.S., France, and other nations eagerly sold him planes, tanks, and artillery.

In spite of Iraq's military buildup, it did not decisively defeat Iran, and in the first months of 1990 the Iraqi economy was still reeling from the effects of the war. Many of its oil facilities, destroyed during the conflict, were still being rebuilt, so some of its vast oil reserves could not be pumped and sold. In addition, Saddam owed a great deal of money to Arab nations that had supported him against Iran. Of Iraq's estimated $80 billion in war debts, half was owed to the Kuwaitis and Saudis.

Why Saddam Coveted Kuwait

The immediate chain of events leading to Saddam's invasion of Kuwait began when he attempted to raise needed income by increasing the price of oil. Early in 1990, he demanded that all OPEC oil producers raise their prices. But some OPEC members, notably Kuwait, refused to raise their prices for fear of losing customers. Without the support of OPEC, Saddam could not raise his own oil prices and this made him increasingly angry with Kuwait.

Saddam also tried to decrease his war debts. He demanded that Kuwait cancel Iraq's debt with the smaller nation, amounting to several billion dollars, saying that the Kuwaitis owed Iraq a heavy measure of gratitude for stopping the Iranians from overrunning Kuwait during the war. In response, the Kuwaitis pointed out that Iran had not tried to overrun Kuwait during that conflict. They simply ignored Saddam's demands and insisted that he pay his war debts.

Convinced that Kuwait had come to stand in the way of Iraq's prosperity, Saddam began seriously considering invading it. His intentions became clear to some Arab leaders a few months before the actual attack. In May 1990, at an Arab conference, Saddam demanded money from the Kuwaitis, and when they bluntly refused, he told an Arab diplomat, "If they don't give it to me, I'm going to take it from them."[8]

In fact, Saddam realized that taking over Kuwait would benefit Iraq in a number of ways. First and foremost, it would allow Iraq to control the rich Kuwaiti oil fields, not only increasing Iraq's wealth but also giving it a stronger voice in setting OPEC oil prices. Controlling Kuwait would also erase Iraq's war debt and give it valuable and strategic ports on the Persian Gulf. In addition, Saddam considered historical reasons for seizing Kuwait, the first being that Iraqi and Kuwaiti tribes had been fighting over the land for centuries. When the

The lights of one of Kuwait's large oil refineries shine like stars in the night.

Kuwaitis had gained their independence in 1961, Iraq had reopened these disputes and laid claim to Kuwait. Iraqi troops had actually threatened to overrun the smaller country, but Britain had intervened and protected the Kuwaitis. Many Iraqis bitterly remembered this episode, believing that Kuwait rightfully belonged to Iraq.

From Saddam's point of view, there seemed to be little military risk involved in seizing Kuwait. First, Kuwait is only about the size of the U.S. state of New Jersey, possessing barely one-twenty-fourth the land area of Iraq. Second, with a population of 2 million, only one-ninth that of Iraq, and an army consisting of only a few thousand men, Kuwait could not adequately defend itself. Also, Saddam expected little opposition to the takeover of Kuwait from either Arab or Western countries. Most Arabs disapproved of Kuwait's emir (royal ruler), Jaber al-Ahmad al Sabah, and his family, so it seemed safe to assume that other Arab nations would not come to the aid of Kuwait. Saddam reasoned that Western countries like the United States were mainly interested in defending Israel and would not get involved in a dispute between Arabs. He also recalled that the U.S., France, and other Western nations had supplied him with arms to fight Iran. He believed that this made him an ally of the West and assumed that U.S. and Western support for his regime would continue even after a takeover of Kuwait.

Saddam: Both Knight and Executioner

Saddam Hussein was born in 1937 into a poor Iraqi family. In his teens, he joined the Ba'ath party, which was trying to get control of the Iraqi government. When he was twenty-two, Saddam, whose name means "one who confronts," took part in a machine-gun attack on the car carrying the country's president, Abdul-Karem Kassim. The Ba'athists hoped to eliminate Kassim and seize power. Although the assassination attempt failed, the Ba'athists managed to gain power in the 1960s and Saddam quickly rose through the ranks, becoming one of the party's chief negotiators. After becoming Iraq's leader in 1979, he carried on the Ba'athist policy of harsh dictatorship, and Middle Eastern experts soon called his regime one of the most brutal and repressive in the world. They noted how he maintained his power by exiling people, arresting and detaining them without trials, and torturing and executing them. According to a former Israeli intelligence officer, Saddam is a practical person who "lacks the usual morals common to human beings."

Morals aside, Saddam used his power and money to project a fatherly, heroic image to his people. He ordered that huge paintings and sculptures of himself adorn public squares and buildings. He also called himself the modern successor of the kings of Babylon and the "Knight of the Arab Nation," the supposed future leader of the entire Arab world, and the result was that many Iraqis came to idolize him. "Saddam, we will give our blood for you!" goes the refrain of a popular Iraqi children's song. Some Iraqi artists used their own blood to paint his portrait, and Iraqi newspapers declared him to be "the anchor and hope of the meek and the weak." But while Iraqis heaped praises on Saddam, he continued to rule with an iron fist. In the late 1980s, in an attempt to suppress those few who dared to protest his rule, he used chemical weapons on his own people.

This painting of Saddam emphasizes his self-proclaimed role as "Knight and Executioner."

Kuwait's ruler, Emir Sheik Jaber al-Ahmad al Sabah, who escaped his country during the Iraqi invasion.

A Barrage of Insults and Threats

The first stage of Saddam's campaign against Kuwait was a series of verbal attacks, made up mostly of exaggerations and outright lies designed to make Kuwait look bad to other Arabs. On July 17, 1990, for example, he publicly threatened the use of force against the Kuwaitis if they did not agree to raise oil prices. Kuwaiti refusals to do so, said Saddam, were part of a "plot" hatched between the Americans and Kuwaitis. Their plan, he charged, was to afford the United States a cheap flow of oil, make the Kuwaitis richer than they already were, and hurt other Arab economies. In a speech on Iraqi television, Saddam gave notice to the Kuwaitis, saying,

> If words fail to protect Iraqis, something effective must be done to return things to their natural course and return usurped [stolen] rights to their owners. . . . Iraqis will not forget the maxim [old saying] that cutting necks is better than cutting the means of living. Oh God Almighty, be witness that we have warned them.[9]

The day after Saddam's TV speech, Iraq's foreign minister, Tarik Aziz, delivered a letter to the Arab League charging that Kuwait was involved in a Western-supported Zionist plot designed to depress oil prices and bankrupt other Arab nations in the Middle East. According to Aziz, the Zionists wanted to weaken the Arabs so that Arab nations could no longer threaten Israel. He also claimed that the Kuwaitis had stolen $2.4 billion worth of oil, over a period of ten years, from an Iraqi oil field near the border between the two countries. One way or another, said Aziz, the Kuwaitis would pay for their treachery. And even as he spoke, large numbers of Iraqi troops were already beginning to move toward the Kuwaiti border.

In response to these trumped-up charges, Kuwaiti spokesmen emphatically denied the existence of an oil plot and insisted that their country had never stolen oil from anyone. Alarmed at Iraq's warlike stance, the Kuwaiti emir dispatched messengers to the Arab capitals of the region to ask for their assistance if Iraq attacked his country. He also put Kuwait's twenty-thousand-man army on full alert.

There was good reason for this precaution. By July 23, 1990, more than 100,000 Iraqi soldiers had massed along the Iraqi-Kuwaiti border. Saddam tried to make this troop buildup look innocent by insisting that his army posed no threat to Kuwait. "We don't want war," he told some foreign diplomats in Baghdad. "We hate war. We know what war does."[10] On July 24, Saddam assured Egypt's president, Hosni Mubarak, that he had no intention of invading Kuwait and repeated the same message to the U.S. ambassador to Iraq. Because they took Saddam at his word, these diplomats, along with most world leaders, were surprised and shocked when Iraqi tanks rolled into Kuwait only one week later.

Kuwait Is Overrun

At 2:00 A.M. on August 2, 1990, the Iraqi army launched a sudden and massive attack on Kuwait. Tens of thousands of Iraqi soldiers poured over the border and quickly overwhelmed a small force of Kuwaiti border guards, Kuwait's only line of defense against invasion. The Iraqi troops were supported by thousands of tanks, armored vehicles, and artillery pieces. The invaders moved swiftly down the six-lane highway leading to Kuwait City, the country's capital and home to two-thirds of its people. Most Kuwaitis were still asleep, but Kuwaiti lookout stations flashed warnings of the invasion to the royal palace. Thus alerted, Kuwaiti leaders tried valiantly to organize a defense of the city, but they had too few troops and much too little time.

It was still dark when Iraqi soldiers reached the capital. Small groups of Kuwaiti soldiers and civilians armed with rifles opened fire on the invaders, but these brave resisters were no match for the Iraqi

The Tiny but Rich Nation of Kuwait

For a thousand years, the flat deserts of Kuwait were the home of nomadic tribes of Arab herders and fishers called Bedouins. (The Bedouins still exist in Kuwait and other areas of the Middle East.) In the early 1700s, the Anaiza tribe founded the city of Kuwait, which means "the little fortress" in Arabic, near the shores of the Persian Gulf. A ruling family, the Sabahs, soon came to power. Every leader (called an emir) of Kuwait since that time has been a member of the Sabah family. One of the most important emirs, Mubarak al-Sabah, signed a treaty with Britain in 1899, making Kuwait a British protectorate (meaning that Britain handled Kuwait's foreign affairs and protected it against aggression). When oil was discovered in Kuwait in the 1930s, everyday life began to change. Most Kuwaitis gave up herding, fishing, and pearl diving and became involved in some aspect of oil production. By the 1980s, thanks to hefty oil profits, Kuwait had become one of the world's richest nations. Most Kuwaiti citizens enjoy comfortable lives supported by generous government benefits and privileges. Abundant wealth allows many Kuwaitis to hire foreign servants and workers, most of these from Egypt, India, Pakistan, and Iran.

Egypt's president, Hosni Mubarak, pictured at left, quickly condemned Saddam's takeover of Kuwait. Below, members of Saddam's Republican Guard stand on their tank, which has just damaged the Kuwaiti mosque seen behind them.

tanks and armored vehicles that blasted away at buildings, cars, and practically anything that moved. As the Iraqis neared the palace, the emir loaded his family into a helicopter. He felt that the best thing he could do for his country at that point was to keep the leadership intact and seek outside help. Amid the gunfire and explosions of the ongoing battle, the helicopter lifted off, banked low over the gulf, and sped southward toward Saudi Arabia. Meanwhile, the emir's younger brother elected to stay behind to command the palace guards, who continued to resist the attack. All of these men died less than an hour later in a courageous but futile defense of the palace.

During the morning and afternoon of August 2, Kuwaiti troops and armed civilians continued as best as they could to resist the huge Iraqi war machine. But their situation was hopeless. Units of Kuwait's tiny army were scattered across the country and could not be organized into an effective fighting force. Moreover, these troops had only minimal military training and no battle experience. By contrast, the Iraqi troops who were spearheading the invasion were members of Saddam's Republican Guard. His best soldiers, they were well trained, and most of them had seen action in the Iraq-Iran war. The Kuwaitis also faced large portions of Iraq's formidable force of some 5,500 tanks. Almost all of Kuwait's 275 tanks had been captured by the Iraqis in the first few hours of the invasion. Thus, by the end of the first day the invaders had managed to crush resistance in Kuwait City and other key towns, completing the takeover of Kuwait.

As these events were unfolding, leaders in Saudi Arabia, shocked and angered at Saddam's attack on fellow Arabs, immediately offered protection to the Kuwaiti emir and his family. The emir ordered the Kuwaiti ambassador to the United Nations to inform the world about Iraq's aggression. He also opened a communications link with the United States and pleaded with American authorities to help his country. Next, the emir delivered a dramatic radio address. He spoke directly to his people, but the speech contained clear warnings to Iraq. "Let them take the chalice [cup] of death," he said. "They have come to kill the sons of Kuwait and its women. We shall fight them everywhere until we clean their treachery from our land. . . . The entire world is with us!"[11] As world leaders began expressing their outrage over Iraq's actions, it became clear that the emir had not been exaggerating.

Global Reactions to the Iraqi Invasion

Indeed, most countries immediately condemned the Iraqi takeover of Kuwait. U.S. response was especially strong; President George Bush called the Iraqi move "naked

This photo, taken through the window of a passing car, shows Iraqi troops riding on one of their tanks two days after they invaded Kuwait.

aggression" and ordered U.S. economic sanctions (penalties) against Iraq. His intention was to persuade Saddam to leave Kuwait by hurting the Iraqis financially. First, Bush froze the $20 billion of Iraqi money then deposited in U.S. banks, making it impossible for the Iraqis to withdraw or earn interest on their money. Britain and France, whose banks also contained large sums of Iraqi money, did the same. Next, Bush banned all U.S. imports of Iraqi oil, which constituted approximately 4 percent of total U.S. oil consumption.

President Bush did not stop with these economic sanctions. As a warning to the Iraqis to leave Kuwait, he ordered an aircraft carrier, the USS *Independence*, into the Persian Gulf. There, the vessel joined eight other U.S. warships that had guarded oil tankers during the Iraq-Iran war. Saddam reacted defiantly to Bush's moves. "We swear,"

An American fighter plane prepares for a catapult launch from the deck of the aircraft carrier USS Independence, *one of several U.S. ships sent to the Persian Gulf.*

the Iraqi leader threatened, "that we will make the Gulf a graveyard for all those who think of committing aggression, starting with those cowardly American navies."[12]

Ignoring Saddam's threats, numerous other countries joined the United States in calling for Iraq to get out of Kuwait. The United Nations convened an emergency session on the evening of August 2, only hours after the fall of Kuwait. The fifteen-member Security Council, the U.N.'s decision-making branch, passed a resolution condemning Iraq and demanding that it withdraw its troops immediately. Only Yemen, an Arab country sympathetic to Iraq, refused to vote. The council also warned that U.N.-sponsored economic sanctions might be used if Iraq did not comply. The Soviet Union was among the countries that voted yes to the resolution, a move many people found surprising since in the past the Soviets had sold the Iraqis more weapons than any other country. In addition to voting to condemn the invasion, the Soviets suspended all arms shipments to Iraq, calling for "a swift and unconditional withdrawal of Iraqi forces from Kuwaiti territory."[13]

In an even more unexpected move, the next afternoon the United States and the Soviet Union issued a joint statement, something the two rival superpowers had never done before. U.S. secretary of state James Baker and Soviet foreign minister Eduard Shevardnadze strongly condemned what they called "the brutal and illegal invasion of Kuwait." They added, "Today, we take the unusual step of jointly calling upon the rest of the international community to join with us in an international cutoff of all arms supplies to Iraq."[14] This joint statement was significant, for the crisis had given the two superpowers, who normally opposed each other in the Middle East, a common cause in the region. Some diplomats suggested that this might make future problems in the area easier to solve.

Waiting for Saddam's Next Move

Regarding the immediate problem in the area, many world leaders worried that Saddam's aggression might not stop with Kuwait. Saudi leaders, for example, privately warned the United States and other Western countries that Saudi Arabia might well be Iraq's next target. Although militarily stronger than the Kuwaitis, the Saudis had little chance against Iraq's army, which most Western experts called the fourth largest in the world. The Saudis and others argued that Saddam was trying to corner the world oil market. Taking Kuwait, they explained, gave him control of 20 percent of the world's oil, and if he got his hands on the vast Saudi oil fields, he would control 45 percent. Many Arabs, like Saad Jabr, an Iraqi politician living in exile in London, warned that Saddam should not be trusted. "Knowing Saddam," Jabr declared, "if in 30 days nothing happens except verbal threats, he will take over the eastern part of Saudi Arabia [where the oil fields are located]. . . . And if anyone moves against him, he will threaten to blow it up."[15]

U.S. Secretary of State James Baker (above), and Soviet foreign minister Eduard Shevardnadze, who tried to achieve a diplomatic solution.

All this talk about a possible Iraqi attack on Saudi Arabia created tension in the United States. Many Americans worried that President Bush might decide to send U.S. troops to defend the Saudi oil fields, and they feared that such a move might escalate the crisis and eventually engulf the region in a bloody war. In such a war, according to this view, tens of thousands of Americans might die, as they had in the Vietnam conflict.

Fear of such a potentially disastrous conflict was certainly not restricted to the United States. Government leaders around the world debated what to do about the Iraqi invasion. Saddam's aggression had created a dangerous international crisis, which, some Arab diplomats pointed out, was something Saddam had not expected when he launched his invasion. To save face, they predicted, he would likely refuse to bend to the many demands that he get out of Kuwait. He might even take the drastic step of annexing (attaching) the tiny country, making it just another part of Iraq. The world community would then be left with two painful choices. It could turn its back and abandon the Kuwaitis to their tragic fate, or it could use military force to drive the Iraqis out of Kuwait. Either way, a good deal of uncertainty and human suffering undoubtedly lay ahead.

★ Chapter 3 ★

"Desert Shield": The World Against Iraq

Saddam Hussein had not expected such a huge international outcry against his takeover of Kuwait. And his invasion of that nation ended up badly hurting his image, especially with countries that had once supported him, such as the United States, the Soviet Union, and France. But in Saddam's view, to retreat immediately from Kuwait, as world opinion demanded, would only further damage his image. Although most nations now looked on him as an aggressor, he reasoned, backing down would make him look weak and cowardly in their eyes. And this would surely destroy his credibility with Middle Eastern Arabs like the Jordanians and Palestinians, who looked to him as a strong leader who could stand up to any odds. Saddam therefore chose to hold onto Kuwait, gambling that the world community would eventually tire of protesting and that in time the crisis would fade.

But Saddam's stubborn refusal to vacate Kuwait had exactly the opposite effect than the one he had hoped for. In the eyes of most other nations, the takeover of Kuwait set a very dangerous precedent. If they allowed Saddam to hold onto his prize, he might attack other countries; moreover, other dictators around the world would get the message that they could attack their neighbors without fear of international police action. The world community had another reason for taking strong action against Saddam, namely that his invasion had placed him in a position to control much of the Middle Eastern oil market. Conceivably, he might later use this power as a weapon to hurt the economies of other nations. So instead of fading, as Saddam had hoped it would, the crisis intensified for many months as members of the world community took nonviolent steps to attempt to force the Iraqis out of Kuwait.

The United Nations Takes Action

The U.N. Security Council took the first step against Saddam on August 2, 1990.

How George Bush Learned to Deal with Bullies

Born in 1924 in Milton, Massachusetts, George Herbert Walker Bush enlisted in the U.S. Navy in the early days of World War II. At age eighteen he was, for a time, the youngest American fighter pilot. During the Pacific conflict, he flew fifty-eight combat missions and was rescued by a submarine after being shot down. After the war, Bush attended Yale University, graduating with a degree in economics in 1948. He then became an executive for a Texas-based oil company.

In 1966, Bush entered politics, winning a Texas seat in the U.S. House of Representatives. In 1971, President Richard Nixon appointed him U.S. ambassador to the United Nations, where, among other things, Bush argued for the presence of an international peacekeeping force in the Middle East. Although he supported Nixon, he had the courage to ask him to resign when it became clear that Nixon had lied during the Watergate scandal. Bush then served as ambassador to China and as head of the Central Intelligence Agency (CIA) under President Ford. Bush ran for the Republican nomination for president in 1980 but lost to Ronald Reagan, after which Reagan asked him to become his running mate. In two terms as vice president, Bush traveled to more than sixty countries and headed task forces fighting crime, terrorism, and drug smuggling.

While running for president in 1988, Bush called for the establishment of a "kinder, gentler nation." After winning the election and becoming the nation's forty-first president, he worked to improve relations with the Soviet Union and also ordered American troops into Panama to depose its dictator, Manuel Noriega, and restore the government elected by the Panamanian people. Eight months later, Bush found himself facing off with another foreign dictator when Saddam Hussein invaded Kuwait. Many journalists have pointed out that Bush's old-fashioned American upbringing shaped his attitudes about dealing with international criminals and bullies. Commented *Newsweek*'s Evan Thomas, "Bush is a product of a culture that prized not only good breeding and proper manners, but. . . [also physical strength and moral courage]. As a child, Bush was taught to play fair, but he was also taught to punch a bully in the nose."

A young George Bush poses proudly in his World War II torpedo bomber. He was shot down but fortunately was rescued.

The U.N. demanded in no uncertain terms that the Iraqi leader pull his troops out of Kuwait and threatened to impose economic sanctions on Iraq if he refused. Security Council members then waited four days for him to comply. During that time, Saddam showed no sign whatsoever of beginning an Iraqi withdrawal. In fact, there were reports filtering out of Kuwait of Iraqi soldiers looting stores and shooting

Kuwaiti citizens. So council members came to the conclusion that they had no choice but to impose the previously threatened sanctions.

On August 6, the council voted on and approved a sweeping trade embargo against Iraq. U.N. Resolution 661 called for all countries immediately to halt all trade with Iraq and to stop any financial and commercial dealings with the Iraqis. The resolution stated in part,

> All states [nations] shall prevent: (a) the import into their territories of all the commodities and products originating in Iraq or Kuwait exported therefrom after the date of the present resolution; (b) any activities by their nationals or in their territories which would promote or are calculated to promote the export . . . of any commodities or products from Iraq or Kuwait; and any dealings by their nationals or their flag vessels . . . including in particular any transfer of funds to Iraq or Kuwait for the purpose of such activities or dealings; (c) the sale or supply by their nationals . . . of any commodities or products, including weapons or any other military equipment . . . but not including supplies intended strictly for medical purposes, and, in humanitarian circumstances, foodstuffs, to any person or body in Iraq or Kuwait. . . . All states shall not make available to the Government of Iraq or to any commercial, industrial or public facility undertaking in Iraq or Kuwait, any funds or any other financial or economic resources and shall prevent their nationals and any persons within their territories from removing from their territories . . . such funds or resources . . . except payments exclusively for strictly medical or humanitarian purposes.[16]

This action was both dramatic and significant in that it marked only the third time in the U.N.'s history that the organization

Iraqi women protest the U.N. embargo against their country. Though unavoidable, the blockade hurt many of Iraq's poor.

had imposed sanctions on a member country. Furthermore, the sanctions against Iraq were by far the most severe the U.N. had ever imposed. The goal was simple: to make the Iraqis leave Kuwait by hurting them in the pocketbook. Within mere hours, Iraq felt the first effects of these sanctions, as the Turks shut down the pipeline that carried Iraqi oil through Turkey to foreign markets.

The U.N. embargo constituted clear evidence that the international community was willing to take necessary and substantial steps against Iraq. And this was the kind of support that President Bush needed to justify sending troops to deal with the situation. Many world leaders believed that the sanctions by themselves were not enough to prevent an Iraqi takeover of Saudi Arabia. Indeed, Bush, as well as British, French, Saudi, and other leaders, felt that U.S. troops should be stationed in Saudi Arabia to send a clear and strong signal to Saddam that an assault on the Saudis would not be tolerated. The same leaders also concurred that the sanctions would be all the more effective if they were accompanied by a show of military force. With world opinion now firmly on his side, therefore, Bush decided to act.

Marshalling U.S. Forces

On August 6, 1990, the same day that the embargo against Iraq took effect, President Bush announced that he was ordering troops to Saudi Arabia. "This will not stand," he angrily told the American press. "This will not stand, this aggression against Kuwait." The president acknowledged that sending in the U.S. military was a calculated risk, but he declared firmly that there was no choice. He said that he intended "to stand up for what's right and condemn what's wrong."[17]

Bush dubbed the defense of Saudi Arabia Operation "Desert Shield." He immediately mobilized more than 50,000 U.S. troops and ordered that at least 100,000 more prepare to ship out. Within hours, squadrons of F-15 fighter planes and paratroopers from the Eighty-second Airborne Division were on their way to the Middle East. In addition, special radar-equipped planes called AWACs and huge B-52 bombers fueled up and headed toward Saudi Arabia, along with large numbers of deadly F-111 fighter bombers stationed in England and Turkey.

At the same time, the massive aircraft carrier USS *Eisenhower* and its escort warships, stationed in the Mediterranean, went into action, moving quickly through the Suez Canal and into the Red Sea. This placed the carrier's attack planes within striking distance of Iraqi targets. Meanwhile, the carrier *Saratoga* and its escorts left Florida, bound for the Persian Gulf. Accompanying them was the battleship *Wisconsin,* carrying cruise missiles, computer-guided weapons that fly only a few hundred feet above ground level and strike with unusual accuracy.

Many countries, including England, France, and Saudi Arabia, publicly praised

An American warplane flies over Saudi Arabia, while a helicopter door gunner watches the USS Eisenhower *pass through the Suez Canal.*

Bush's strong show of military force. But some government leaders, including several U.S. congressmen, were worried. They warned that a confrontation between the Americans and Iraqis might provoke Saddam to attack U.S. forces and perhaps Israel too, in which case the Middle East would be engulfed by full-scale war. In fact, the world marketplace reflected this fear of war. To cover themselves in case Middle Eastern oil supplies became scarce, for example, oil companies around the world sharply raised their prices. At the same time, financial markets such as the New York Stock Exchange were unsure of how a war might affect the value of oil and other commodities, and a flurry of panic buying and selling made these markets temporarily unstable. Attempting to ease these fears, President Bush stated that his aim was not to provoke a war. "Four simple principles guide our policy," he explained.

> First, we seek the immediate, unconditional, and complete withdrawal of all Iraqi forces from Kuwait. Second, Kuwait's legal government must be restored. . . . And third, my administration, as has been the case with every president from President Roosevelt to President Reagan, is committed to the security and stability of the Persian Gulf. And fourth, I am determined to protect the lives of American citizens abroad.[18]

A Split in the Arab World

As might be expected, Saddam Hussein reacted defiantly to President Bush's military buildup in Saudi Arabia. First, Saddam tried to appeal to his many Arab supporters in the Middle East. Attempting to make it appear that U.S. troops were there expressly to harm Arabs, he threatened to "pluck out the eyes of those who attack the Arab nation."[19] Then, on August 8, 1990, Saddam boldly announced that Iraq had formally annexed Kuwait, a move that expert Western observers had expected the dictator to make as he dug in his heels to resist the forces gathering against him. To justify this brazen action, as well as the invasion itself, in the eyes of his fellow Arabs, Saddam invented a story designed to make it appear that he was actually helping the Kuwaitis. He claimed that the Kuwaiti people had overthrown their "corrupt" emir and begged for Iraq to aid them. In this bogus scenario, the Kuwaitis fervently desired to return to the "mother homeland" of Iraq. "Thank God," Saddam said, "that we are now one people, one state that will be the pride of the Arabs."[20] Not accepting this story, most members of the world community quickly condemned the annexation of Kuwait, and by a vote of fifteen to zero, the U.N. Security Council declared that annexation null and void.

Saddam's Arab supporters, on the other hand, expressed their approval of his actions against Kuwait and vowed to help him against the United States. These supporters represented a minority of Arabs. Indeed, a large portion of the Arab world was shocked and horrified by Saddam's attack on and annexation of Kuwait. Voicing the opinion of many Arabs, Saudi Arabia's King Fahd called the Iraqi invasion "the most vile aggression known to the Arab nation in its modern history." He tried to reassure Arabs who feared the presence of U.S. troops in the Middle East, saying that these forces, "are here to help defend the kingdom [of Saudi Arabia] . . . and will leave as soon as the kingdom so demands."[21]

Resentment

Many other Arabs who opposed Iraq's policies, including the Egyptians, had resented Saddam even before the invasion of Kuwait. Prior to Iraq's 1980s military buildup, Egypt had been the strongest, most influential country in the Middle East, and Arabs had looked on Egypt's capital of Cairo as the region's most important city. Consequently, the Egyptians were offended by Saddam's attempts to make his own capital of Baghdad the political center and heart of the Middle East. Immediately after Iraq annexed Kuwait on August 8, Egypt's president Mubarak ordered Egyptian troops to Saudi Arabia to back up the Americans. "If anyone [i.e., Saddam] starts attacking," he warned, "we are ready to confront him."[22] This marked the first time in history that Arabs had joined with outsiders to confront other Arabs. And Egypt was not alone. Syria also sent troops to help defend the Saudis against Saddam, as did Morocco (an Arab nation located in north Africa).

These countries harshly criticized Saddam at an August 10 emergency meeting of the Arab League in Cairo. The Iraqi dictator immediately countered them with a

Saudi Arabia's King Fahd, who called Saddam's invasion "a vile aggression."

bitter verbal attack that shocked many Arabs. Sending a message from his palace in Baghdad, he called on Arabs and Muslims to begin a bloody jihad against all foreign troops and "corrupt" Arab rulers. Saddam tried to incite the jihad with the false and patently ridiculous claim that the Americans and Zionists had captured the holy city of Mecca, calling on his followers to "burn the land under the feet of the aggressive invaders."[23]

Egyptian, Syrian, Saudi, and other Arab leaders swiftly rejected Saddam's words, calling them warlike and misguided. Arab League delegates from Egypt and other moderate Arab states drafted a resolution denouncing the annexation of Kuwait, endorsing U.N. sanctions against Iraq, and calling for the creation of an Arab military force to keep the peace. Of the twenty-one members of the league, twelve voted in favor of the resolution. Of the remaining members, Iraq, Libya, and the PLO voted no, and the other six refused to vote. Thus, although the Arab League had made an official stand against Iraq, the voting indicated that a sizable minority of Arabs still backed Saddam.

Saddam Threatens His Enemies

After the Arab League's vote, Saddam adopted still another threatening posture, this time announcing that Iraq would never leave Kuwait unless the Israelis withdrew from the territories they had occupied in the 1967 and 1973 wars. Western and Arab officials saw this as his attempt to bolster his image with the Arab masses, who still bitterly resented Israel. Apparently, Saddam believed that linking his takeover of Kuwait with the Israeli issue would win him the support of most Arabs. But moderate Arabs, like the Egyptians and Saudis, as well as the Western nations, rejected this "linkage" ploy outright, insisting

Worries About Iraq's Chemical Weapons

As the likelihood of war in the Middle East increased in the last months of 1990, Americans and their allies worried about Iraq's arsenal of chemical weapons. After a series of horrifying gas attacks during World War I, world leaders came to view using poison gases on people as unusually cruel and inhumane; so they outlawed chemical weapons in the 1925 Geneva Protocol. However, this treaty did not prohibit nations from producing and stockpiling such weapons. In the 1980s, Western intelligence reports indicated that the Iraqis had amassed between two thousand and four thousand tons of chemical weapons. Moreover, in an attempt to both cripple and terrorize the enemy, Saddam used poison gas against the Iranians in the Iraq-Iran war. He also unleashed such weapons on the Kurds, Iraq's largest ethnic minority (who live mainly in northern Iraq), to suppress Kurdish protests and rebellions. In the fall of 1990, some Iraqi diplomats warned that Saddam would not hesitate to use the same weapons on Americans or other "foreign invaders" who posed a threat to Iraq. Preparing for the worst, therefore, U.S. commanders began supplying gas masks and special protective suits to all U.S. troops and personnel heading for the Middle East.

American troops don gas masks and other gear designed to repel chemical weapons. There were real fears that Saddam might use such weapons.

that the two issues were separate. The idea of linkage between Kuwait and Israel, an Egyptian official said, went against "what the Arab and Islamic nations had agreed [to] unanimously, namely an immediate Iraqi withdrawal from Kuwait."[24] Syrian officials were more blunt:

> The appalling attempt to link the Iraqi withdrawal from Kuwait and the Israeli withdrawal from the occupied Arab territories [is a gross falsehood]. After all, how can we equate Kuwait, the fraternal Arab country, with Israel, the Arab arch-enemy? Every Arab citizen knows that when Arab countries invade each other Israel will celebrate and perpetuate its occupation of the Arab lands. Linking withdrawal from Kuwait to Israel's withdrawal from the occupied

> Arab territories, therefore, is not only a falsehood but also a weak excuse for the continuation of the invasion.[25]

In general, the Arab representatives held that Saddam's attempt at linkage was nothing more than a desperate move that served only to inflame the crisis initiated by Iraq.

Angered by all of this international condemnation, Saddam and other Iraqi officials threatened to destroy any armies, Arab or otherwise, that dared to interfere in Iraq's business. Other warnings from Baghdad followed, some directed specifically at the Americans and other Westerners. One issue that concerned world leaders was that the Iraqi spokesmen who issued these warnings refused to rule out Iraq's possible use of chemical weapons if attacked. Western officials did not take this threat lightly, for they recalled that Saddam had employed poison gas attacks on the Iranians in the 1980s in open violation of international laws against the use of such weapons.

Saddam also warned that his Muslim supporters would help Iraq by striking at its enemies around the world. This was a clear reference to terrorist groups that had committed acts of violence against the West before. One worried U.S. official predicted, "If we push this guy [Saddam] too hard, bombs will go off in Europe."[26] Addressing this concern, a week after the invasion of Kuwait the U.S. State Department issued a warning to Americans about "the risk of terrorist incidents directed against American interests overseas."[27]

Another ominous Iraqi threat concerned the fate of foreigners living in or visiting Iraq and Kuwait. These included approximately thirty-five hundred Americans, five thousand British, and several thousand citizens of France, the Soviet Union, and other countries. One of Saddam's ministers warned, "Countries that resort to. . . [war against] Iraq should remember they have interests and nationals [citizens] in Kuwait."[28] In the United States, State Department phones were jammed with calls from worried relatives of Americans who were living in or visiting the Middle East. U.S. diplomats accordingly worked day and night trying to make contact with Americans stranded in Kuwait.

The Crisis Worsens

On August 17, 1990, the Iraqis acted on their threat against the foreign nationals. U.S., British, and other foreign citizens were not allowed to leave Iraq or Kuwait, and an Iraqi spokesman said that the nationals would stay "as long as Iraq remains threatened with an aggressive war."[29] Saddam claimed that he would free the foreigners if and when the United States got out of Saudi Arabia and soon afterward announced that Iraq had begun moving Westerners to key military and industrial sites. This, he said, was to discourage the U.S. from bombing Iraqi targets. The use of hostages as "human shields" against attack outraged most nations, and the U.S., Britain, and the other affected countries issued strong protests, saying that taking hostages was a violation of

The Threat of Terrorism

Saddam Hussein's large army and stockpiles of chemical weapons were not the only threats posed to U.S. and Allied forces moving into Saudi Arabia. Saddam also made it clear that, if he was attacked, his supporters would open a "second front" against Western military and civilian targets. He was referring to organized acts of terrorism such as bombings and airplane hijackings. In September and October 1990, known terrorists set up headquarters in Baghdad, and these international criminals enjoyed the support and cooperation of Iraqi authorities. U.S. leaders feared that Arab terrorists might try to attack American military installations as they had in Lebanon in 1983, when a truck carrying explosives slammed into a U.S. barracks, killing 241 American soldiers. To discourage a similar attack in Saudi Arabia, specially trained commandos guarded U.S. and Allied military leaders. These commandos spoke fluent Arabic to help them detect Arab terrorists trying to sneak through the American lines.

American soldiers comb through the rubble following the 1983 bombing of a U.S. military barracks in Lebanon.

international law. Iraq then responded by insisting that the foreigners were not hostages, but only "guests." Said an angry President Bush, "When Saddam Hussein specifically offers to trade the freedom of those citizens of many nations he holds against their will in return for concessions [meeting his demands], there can be little doubt that whatever these innocent people are called, they are in fact hostages."[30]

Whatever Saddam chose to call the people he had detained, it soon became clear that he had once again badly miscalculated the potential effects of his action. As University of Toronto scholar Jean E. Smith puts it,

> Once the hostage issue emerged, whatever international support Saddam may have had quickly evaporated. The heart-rending spectacle of innocent women and children herded into Iraqi holding areas prejudiced even the most sympathetic observer. Saddam, accustomed to bullying his way, had gone too far. France ordered its fleet in the Persian Gulf to cooperate with the U.S. Navy to ensure compliance with U.N.

> sanctions, and within twenty-four hours the [U.N.] Security Council passed a unanimous resolution demanding that Iraq permit the immediate departure of all foreign nationals. This time, both Cuba and Yemen [who had refused to condemn Iraq before] joined the Council's action.[31]

In addition to taking hostages, Saddam ordered all foreign embassies in Kuwait to shut down. Representatives of the United States, Britain, France, the Soviet Union, Germany, Italy, Spain, Denmark, Sweden, and Finland immediately called this demand unacceptable. All refused to close their embassies because they did not recognize the Iraqi takeover of Kuwait as legal. Saddam may have believed that Kuwait was now a part of Iraq rather than an independent nation, but people in other countries saw it quite differently.

The sheer number of nations involved in the embassy-closing incident underscored the scope of the crisis. Indeed, Saddam Hussein's conquest of Kuwait had now become an international problem affecting countries from every part of the globe. All nations were now forbidden to conduct trade with the Iraqis, who had taken hostages in violation of international law and openly threatened terrorism against those who opposed Saddam. As the Middle East moved toward the brink of war, most government leaders were unsure about what the Iraqi dictator might do next. Some U.S. officials remarked that, with the world against him, Saddam's defiant and threatening stance seemed stupid and senseless, and they were not reassured when Tarik Aziz delivered a threat directly aimed at President Bush on August 21. Warned Aziz, "If the American leader thinks that this is a vacation like they had in Panama and Grenada [two small countries that had recently been occupied by U.S. troops], they are mistaken. . . . It will be a bloody conflict, and America will lose and . . . be humiliated."[32]

Chapter 4

The Ominous Prelude to All-Out War

By the beginning of September 1990, most nations had condemned Iraq's takeover of Kuwait. The U.N.'s economic sanctions against Iraq were in effect, and huge numbers of Allied troops continued to pour into Saudi Arabia. Yet in the face of these stern realities, Saddam Hussein still refused to pull his troops out of Kuwait and even showed contempt for world opinion by announcing that he had made Kuwait the nineteenth province of Iraq.

Since it seemed increasingly unlikely that Iraq would give up Kuwait, President George Bush seriously began considering the use of military force. And over the course of a few months he made a number of public remarks warning that time was running out for any credible peaceful solution to the crisis. "There is a ticking of the clock," he told a CNN news reporter in mid-November 1990.

> I don't think this matter is going to go on forever. As far as I am concerned, it's not. . . . If I haven't done as clear a job as I might on explaining this, then I've got to do better in that regard, because I know in my heart of hearts that what we are doing is right. . . . I know that we have to stand up to aggression; an aggression that goes rewarded today means instability and horror tomorrow. . . . When you rape, pillage, and plunder a neighbor, should you then ask the world, hey, give me a little face [i.e., allow me to save face]? The answer is no, there isn't going to be any compromise with this kind of naked aggression.[33]

Such tough words from the commander of the most powerful military establishment on earth were certainly sobering and ominous for most of those who heard them, even if they did not phase Saddam, for they strongly hinted that an all-out, bloody war was practically certain to occur if the Iraqi dictator did not bend to the continuing demands that he vacate Kuwait.

Bush Justifies a War Against Iraq

But talking tough about attacking the Iraqis was one thing and gathering the necessary support to do so was quite another. Bush fully realized that such a large-scale operation would require the support of the American public. But would the American people feel that there was sufficient cause to commit U.S. troops to the Middle East? After all, worries about the potential for another Vietnam-like scenario—a protracted conflict that might result in thousands of American soldiers returning home in body bags—still lingered.

Regarding the burning question of the use of overt force, Bush and his advisers felt that there were several factors that fully justified U.S. military action against Iraq. First, there was intense concern in the United States for the safety of the Kuwaiti people. According to reports trickling out of Kuwait, the Iraqi occupation was brutal and inhumane, and there were confirmed reports of atrocities (acts of unusual violence and cruelty) committed by Iraqi soldiers. People who had managed to escape from Kuwait said they had witnessed Iraqis raping and murdering Kuwaitis, as well as looting and destroying Kuwaiti property. In early October 1990, Dilip Hiro wrote,

In a carefully worded speech, President George Bush warns Saddam that his time is running out.

> The London-based human rights organization Amnesty International produced a report based on evidence collected from scores of interviews with those who had left Kuwait. "Their testimony builds up a horrifying picture of widespread arrests, torture under interrogation, summary executions and mass extra-judicial killings," the report concluded. "Scores of hangings of those suspected of opposing Iraq's annexation of Kuwait have been reported in the grounds of Kuwaiti University. Those hanged were summarily executed without any form of trial after being accused of criminal offenses." These offences included possession of opposition literature, the Kuwaiti flag or a picture of the emir, and refusal to replace the emir's picture with Saddam Hussein's. Some 200 Kuwaitis who had been killed by the Iraqi military had been taken to

> hospitals, where [false] documents certifying that they had died in hospital were obtained by force.[34]

This and other reports about Iraqi atrocities created a palpable feeling of urgency in the United States, as well as in the international community as a whole. And many Americans expressed the view that war with Iraq was the only way to save Kuwait from total destruction.

Another factor that weighed in favor of using force against Iraq was the failure of the U.N. embargo. Iraq's loss of trade was costing it millions of dollars per day, yet the country showed no signs of giving in to this pressure. Moreover, even if the embargo eventually worked, some people argued, it might take years, and by that time Iraq would have completely dismantled and absorbed Kuwait.

In addition, Bush and his advisers considered, Iraq possessed large stores of chemical weapons and possibly biological (germ) weapons. The latter could potentially unleash deadly diseases, such as anthrax and bubonic plague, on Iraq's enemies. There was also ominous evidence that the Iraqis were trying desperately to build nuclear weapons, and they already

The Threat of an Iraqi Atomic Bomb

As tensions in the Middle East increased during the winter of 1990, many world leaders voiced their concerns that Saddam Hussein was in the process of developing nuclear weapons. Many Western scientists claimed that there was nothing to worry about yet, that although Iraq did have a nuclear program, it was still several years away from actually constructing a working atomic bomb. But President Bush was less optimistic. "Every day that passes," he warned, "brings Saddam one step closer to realizing his goal of a nuclear weapons arsenal." Bush's supporters believed that the Iraqis had amassed about three hundred tons of the uranium compounds needed to build atomic bombs. Early in 1990, British agents broke up an Iraqi smuggling ring that tried to sneak Western nuclear trigger devices into Iraq. Citing these facts, Bush insisted that, sooner or later, the Iraqi nuclear program would become a serious threat to peace in the Middle East. Said Bush, "No one knows precisely when this dictator may acquire atomic weapons. But we do know this for sure: He has never possessed a weapon that he didn't use."

For a while, American leaders worried that Saddam might have nuclear weapons like this one, exploded in a U.S. test.

owned Soviet-made missiles that could carry such weapons to other parts of the Middle East, including Israel. Bush and many others in the United States were clearly worried that, once in possession of nuclear weapons, Iraq would be a potent threat to the entire Middle East, for there seemed little doubt in the minds of most Westerners that Saddam Hussein would not hesitate to use such weapons of mass destruction. His brutal takeover of Kuwait and subsequent seizure of thousands of hostages appeared to confirm that he was a ruthless and exceedingly dangerous man. Thus, Bush came to feel that a war against Iraq at that time might deter a larger, more destructive conflict later.

Body bags accumulate in the Vietnam conflict. Many Americans feared that the Iraqi crisis would escalate into another Vietnam.

American Concerns

All of these factors seemed to indicate that the American public would support a U.S. intervention in Iraq. But there were other serious concerns about U.S. military involvement, one of these being the role Israel might play in a U.S. war with Iraq. The United States still strongly supported Israel, and many Americans worried that if the U.S. attacked Iraq, Saddam might retaliate by attacking Israel. If this were to happen, experts on the Middle East said, Israel might retaliate immediately. And if Israel attacked Iraq, the Saudis and other moderate Arabs, still strongly anti-Israel, might then turn on the U.S. and its Western allies. The U.S. would then be faced with a difficult choice: either pull out of the Middle East and abandon Kuwait, or join with the Israelis against all Arabs. A war with all of the Arab nations would certainly be unacceptable to most Americans; therefore, they would likely strongly oppose it. They would also oppose a continuing U.S.-Iraqi conflict that dragged on for months or years.

Americans were concerned about the safety of U.S. soldiers as well. Military action against Iraq would require large numbers of U.S. troops, more than the small regular army could supply. This meant that thousands of reservists (civilians who spend a few weeks each year in basic military training and remain on call in case of a national or other emergency) would have to be called up. Some people worried that there would not be enough time to train the reservists properly for a grueling war in the deserts. By contrast, Iraqi soldiers, who were used to fighting in that region, might have the advantage. In such a scenario, hundreds or even thousands of American soldiers might die, and the sight of Americans coming home in body bags over a foreign war could easily erode public support for U.S. intervention in the Middle East.

There was also the issue of women serving in both the regular army and the reserves. In 1990, more than 11 percent of U.S. forces were women, the highest proportion in the country's history. Women soldiers were not allowed in combat, serving, as military historian Frank Schubert says,

> in jobs generally classified as combat support and combat service support. Combat support assignments, which provided operational help to the combat units, included civil engineering, military police, transporting personnel and equipment via truck or helicopter, communications, and intelligence support. Combat service support positions provided logistical, technical, and ad-

A female U.S. soldier holds her weapon while on guard duty. The possibility of women dying in Iraq worried many Americans.

> ministrative services (such as personnel, postal, medical, and finance) to the combat arm. Female soldiers worked in high concentrations in these areas.[35]

Yet even though women soldiers were not allowed in combat, large numbers of Americans worried that hundreds or thousands of American women might be killed or wounded by Iraqi missiles or bombs falling behind the lines.

Gearing Up for War

As President Bush and other American leaders weighed these pros and cons of war with Iraq, they continued to increase U.S. troop and equipment levels in Saudi Arabia. U.S. armed forces, military bases, factories, and transportation networks mobilized in the largest American military buildup since the Vietnam War. On August 22, 1990, one American official commented that the United States had moved the equivalent of a Midwestern town the size of Fayette, Indiana, to the Persian Gulf in the space of only two weeks. This included 1 billion pounds of arms, ammunition, food, household goods, and water. Dozens of cargo ships and planes worked around the clock, carrying troops and supplies from American bases to the Middle East. Meanwhile, as the buildup continued, the carrier *John F. Kennedy* and several other warships headed for the gulf.

Several other countries increased their military presence in Saudi Arabia during the following two weeks as well. France raised the number of its troops to thirteen thousand and also sent fourteen warships and one hundred antitank helicopters. Britain sent eight thousand troops and 120 tanks. In addition, Secretary of State James Baker and other U.S. and British diplomats convinced many nations to join the growing coalition against Iraq. Responding to this call, Italy, Argentina, and Canada joined the coalition and sent troops, ships, and warplanes. By mid-September, twenty-two nations had joined the coalition of Allies against Iraq, yet this massive buildup of international forces in the Middle East appeared to have little effect on Saddam Hussein. Except for his freeing of about twenty-nine hundred hostages in September 1990, there was no change in the Iraqi position.

Publicly, President Bush expressed the optimistic view that the coalition's enormous display of force would eventually make Saddam back down. But privately, Bush and his advisers were convinced that war with Iraq was inevitable. Accordingly, they met secretly in October and planned an invasion of Iraq and Kuwait, which would tentatively begin in January 1991. Bush's top military advisers informed him that many more troops and arms would be needed for such an operation, and these would take months to transport to the Middle East. So on November 8, 1990, Bush ordered a huge increase in U.S. troop levels in Saudi Arabia. By early 1991, he said, there would be more than 400,000 American soldiers, as well as thousands of American tanks, ships, and

The Apache Helicopter

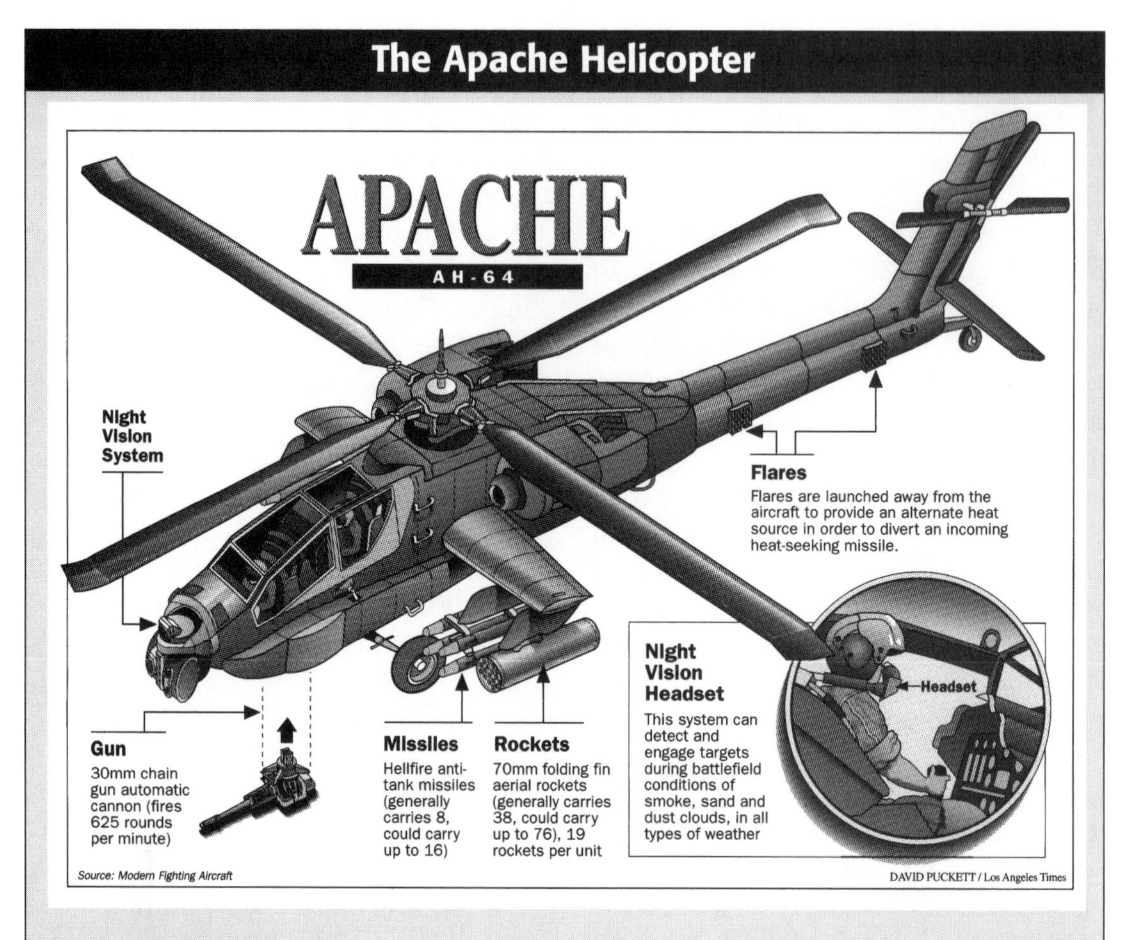

The AH-64 Apache helicopter is one of the U.S. Army's main high-tech antitank weapons and is also designed to provide air support for ground troops. When the troops approach an enemy position, the Apache flies in front of them. The pilot spots the exact positions of enemy soldiers and then fires on them while the attacking troops move in for the kill. Looking something like a giant wasp, the Apache is capable of climbing 3,240 feet per minute and cruises parallel to the ground at 184 miles per hour. The Apache is equipped with some of the most advanced computer and laser systems available, among them an infrared night-vision system allowing the pilot to fly safely at night at low altitudes. The helicopter also has a radar-warning device that tells the pilot when enemy radar has locked on to it. This allows the craft to use evasive maneuvers immediately and escape attack by bullets and missiles. Among the weapons the Apache carries are rapid-firing machine guns, deadly rockets, and powerful antitank missiles with a range of up to five miles. This potentially effective helicopter is not without its faults, however, as shown by problems encountered in deploying it in a European police action in the late 1990s. Critics claimed it took too long to get the Apaches ready for combat; also, some of the craft crashed during training runs, raising concerns about their safety.

fighter planes, involved in Operation Desert Shield. This mobilization of U.S. forces, including the call-up of many reserve units, soon became the largest since World War II.

A Final Warning to Iraq

In preparing U.S. forces for war against Iraq, President Bush realized that the United States could not attack without U.N. approval. After all, the U.S. and other Allies were in Saudi Arabia with the permission of the United Nations, and any military action taken against Iraq would have to have the consent of the majority of the U.N. member nations. Although Bush was already convinced that force would be necessary against Saddam, he needed to convince the U.N. and his allies that this was the case.

Early in November 1990, Bush sent James Baker on an eight-day tour of Europe, Asia, and the Middle East to gain support for the use of force against Iraq. Meeting with the Kuwaiti emir, the British, Chinese, Soviets, Egyptians, Turks, and many others, Baker argued that the sanctions were working slowly and might not persuade the Iraqis to leave Kuwait. He managed to convince all the Allies that they should issue Iraq an ultimatum: Get out of Kuwait by a given date or risk attack by the Allies. On November 7, British prime minister Margaret Thatcher summed up the feelings of most Allied leaders. "Time is running out for Saddam Hussein," she said sternly. "Either he gets out of Kuwait soon or we and our allies will remove him by force and he will go down to defeat with all its consequences. He has been warned."[36]

Baker also took his argument for the use of force against Iraq to the U.N. Security Council. During the debate that followed, the Kuwaiti ambassador delivered an impassioned plea for the U.N. to approve the use of force, calling on the members of the

British prime minister Margaret Thatcher was one of the Allied leaders who gave James Baker their support on his November 1990 European tour.

General Colin Powell

Colin Powell, the top-ranking American general during the Persian Gulf War, is the son of immigrants from the Caribbean island of Jamaica. He grew up in New York City's Harlem district, which is made up almost completely of blacks and other minorities. "When people say to me, 'Weren't you held back?' [because he was black], my simple answer is, 'My color is somebody else's problem and not mine. You just take me as I am.'" Powell believes that America is a place where any person can achieve success through hard work, and he has proved it. He was an honor student in college and then entered the army, where he rose quickly through the ranks. After serving in Vietnam, receiving eleven medals, and commanding dozens of military actions, he became chairman of the joint chief in 1989. Some politicians have called him the "black Eisenhower," comparing him to the famous general who led U.S. and Allied forces in World War II.

U.S. general Colin Powell, the top-ranking American soldier during the Persian Gulf War.

council to save his country from "the atrocities of an Iraqi regime which has run amok."[37] On November 29, the Security Council voted to approve U.N. Resolution 678, authorizing the Allies to use military action against Iraq if it had not pulled out of Kuwait by midnight on January 15, 1991. The vote was thirteen to two, with Yemen and Cuba casting the negative ballots and China abstaining. Just before this vote took place, the Iraqi ambassador to the U.N. predictably condemned the whole proceeding, calling the Security Council "a willing tool of the U.S.," and adding,

> The resolution reflects a double standard by attacking Iraq while allowing Israel to occupy Palestine, and is a plot by Washington to dominate the . . . [Middle] East. The Americans have succeeded in imposing their hegemony [dominance], and their only object is to defend their own and Israel's interests. . . . Iraq wants peace not just for itself but for the whole . . . [Middle] East, including Palestine.[38]

However inaccurate his statement, the Iraqi ambassador had good reason to be upset. The U.N. vote authorizing the use of force was a major victory for Bush, Baker, and other Allied leaders. It marked only the second time in history that the United Nations had approved the use of force against a country. (The first time had been at the beginning of the Korean War in 1950, when the U.N. sponsored military action against the North Koreans.)

Last-Minute Negotiations

Pleased with the U.N.'s authorization of the use of force against Iraq, President Bush lashed out at Saddam, calling the Iraqi leader "a classic bully who thinks he can get away with kicking sand in the face of the world." Bush promised that if force became necessary, "we [the Allies] won't pull any punches."[39] He told the American people that any U.S. action, unlike the fighting in Vietnam, would be swift, massive, and decisive. But he was also careful not to give the impression that he actually wanted a war. On November 30, he offered to send Baker on a peace mission to Baghdad in an effort "to go the extra mile for peace."[40] In this scenario, Iraq's Tarik Aziz could then visit Bush in the United States. After some haggling over locations and dates, U.N. negotiators set up a January 9, 1991, meeting in Geneva, Switzerland, between Baker and Aziz. American leaders held out little hope that this meeting would actually accomplish anything positive. Yet, as Baker put it, "If force ends up being used, we owe it to the American people and to others to show that we left no stone unturned in the search for peace."[41]

Not surprisingly, as the January meeting in Geneva drew closer, tensions around the world increased. Many hoped that Saddam would use the occasion to strike a deal with the Americans and avoid a disastrous war. But Allied military commanders were less optimistic, fearing that Saddam might launch a surprise attack prior to January 15 in an attempt to cripple Allied forces before they were completely prepared. So Allied troops remained on constant alert in case the Iraqi dictator decided to strike.

On January 9, the eyes of the world were trained on Geneva. The meeting lasted several hours, at first raising hopes that Baker and Aziz had achieved a settlement, but these hopes were dashed when the meeting ended in a stalemate. According to Baker, Aziz continued to insist that Iraq would not leave Kuwait until the Israelis gave back the lands taken in the Arab-Israeli wars. Baker said that he "heard nothing that suggested to me any Iraqi flexibility whatsoever. . . . The choice is Iraq's." Baker warned, "If it should choose to continue its brutal occupation of Kuwait, Iraq will be choosing a military confrontation which it cannot win and which will have devastating consequences for Iraq."[42] Aziz countered that the United States did not really want peace. He told Baker that Arabs would refuse to fight Arabs and that in the final moment the Arab members of the Allied forces would abandon the U.S. The Americans would then be left stranded in the desert, where the Iraqis, used to fighting in the sands, would easily defeat them. Aziz also promised that Iraq would attack Israel if the Allies attacked Iraq.

With the failure of the Geneva talks, war between Iraq and the Allies seemed inevitable. But President Bush faced one last obstacle before he could commit U.S. troops to combat. The U.S. Congress had not yet approved the use of force by American soldiers. Beginning on January 8, there was a dramatic four-day-long congressional debate in which Bush's opponents argued that the sanctions should be given more time. They feared another long war like Vietnam, with many U.S. casualties. Asked Senate majority leader George Mitchell, "How many young Americans will die? . . . And the truly haunting question will be: Did they die unnecessarily? For if we go to war now, no one will ever know if the sanctions would have worked."[43]

But Mitchell and those who agreed with him were in the minority. Most lawmakers, like a majority of American citizens, felt that all reasonable efforts for peace had been made and that the threat of military force was the only effective option left. Senator Joseph Lieberman of Connecticut summed up this viewpoint:

Allied soldiers, like this American tank crewman, remained ready to attack at a moment's notice.

> Our final, best chance for a truly peaceful end to this crisis . . . is to send a clear . . . message to Saddam Hussein that the American Congress and the American people stand shoulder to shoulder with our president in this critical moment of confrontation.[44]

Barbara Vucanovich, a Republican from Nevada, added, "There can be no reward for brutal aggression. If we do nothing, and Saddam Hussein pays no price for swallowing up the country of Kuwait. . . we are as guilty as he is."[45] This attitude carried the day. On January 12, Congress voted to approve the use of force if Iraq had not left Kuwait by the U.N. deadline.

In the final three days before that deadline, both the president of France and the U.N. secretary general tried to reason with Saddam. But they failed to convince him that a war against the Allies would be disastrous for Iraq. If the Americans got involved, Saddam boasted, the Iraqis would make them swim in their own blood. President Bush responded by telling some congressional leaders, "If we get into an armed situation, [Saddam] is going to get his ass kicked."[46] This last-minute bout of verbal sparring by the two leaders left millions around the world with the feeling that there was no way war could be avoided. The burning question was: When the deadline came and the clock struck twelve, who would strike first?

Chapter 5

"Desert Storm": The Massive Allied Air Assault

As the last minutes before the January 15, 1991, U.N. deadline ticked away, both Iraqi and Allied forces stood ready. Tens of thousands of Iraqi troops peered out from trenches and concrete bunkers constructed in the desert along the Kuwaiti-Saudi border. Tense and worried, they wondered whether the Allies would attack exactly at midnight or prolong the agony by waiting. Meanwhile, at the huge Allied air base at Dhahran, on the Saudi coast about two hundred miles south of Kuwait, radar operators kept a watchful eye on their screens. They knew that an attack by Iraqi planes or missiles could come at any moment. Not far away on the same base, Allied pilots stood by in their flight suits, awaiting the order to board their planes.

In Israel, the mood was equally tense, as Israeli pilots sat in the cockpits of their jets twenty-four hours a day. If the signal came, they could be airborne in just seconds and on their way to bomb Iraqi targets. Although Israel was not a member of the Allied coalition, Israeli leaders took Saddam's threat to attack their country very seriously. (The U.S. had excluded Israel from the coalition to avoid possible friction with Arab members.) President Bush had privately asked Israeli leaders to show restraint if attacked, but they had not assured him that they would do so; they had insisted that any decision about retaliation would have to be made when and if the Iraqis actually attacked them.

In the United States and a number of other countries, many people could not sleep. In fact, millions of people sat before their televisions, waiting for the expected news bulletin announcing the beginning of hostilities. Yet when midnight of the target date came, that bulletin did not. To the surprise of most observers, the deadline passed uneventfully, and as the morning and afternoon of January 16 dragged on without any news of fighting in the Middle East, many people breathed a sigh of relief. Perhaps,

An American F-14 Tomcat fighter prepares to take off from the USS John F. Kennedy *on a bombing run over Iraq.*

they thought optimistically, there would be no war after all. Some theorized that President Bush and other Allied leaders had been bluffing all along about using force and that Saddam had called their bluff.

It soon became clear, however, that the Allies had not been bluffing. At a few minutes past 7:00 P.M. (Eastern Standard Time) in the evening of Wednesday, January 16, the bulletin that so many people had been dreading finally came. President Bush's spokesman, Marlin Fitzwater, announced to the press that Allied planes had begun bombing Iraqi targets at 4:50 that afternoon (12:50 A.M. on January 17 in Iraq and Kuwait). The operation had been dubbed "Desert Storm," Fitzwater said, adding that "the liberation of Kuwait has begun."[47]

Blinding the Iraqi Defenses

Desert Storm was, without question, the largest air assault in history. Its goal was to make it impossible for Iraq to attack Saudi Arabia and also to weaken the Iraqi army in preparation for a later Allied ground assault to liberate Kuwait. Allied planes were on a mission to destroy Iraqi airfields, missile sites, troop bunkers, army bases, weapons factories, and industrial facilities. The Allies would also strike communications and transportation networks in order to confuse and disrupt Iraqi defensive efforts. At the same time, the planes would bomb as many of Iraq's chemical, biological, and nuclear facilities as possible so that the Iraqis would thereafter be unable to threaten their neighbors with these weapons of mass destruction. The locations of all Iraqi targets had been pinpointed and mapped by special cameras aboard U.S. satellites and high-flying spy planes.

In the opening of the assault, hundreds of Allied planes roared off runways in Saudi Arabia and from the decks of carriers in the Red Sea and Persian Gulf. As they converged on Iraq and occupied Kuwait, the first step in the Allied plan—the elimination of Iraqi radar defenses—began. This was essential to the success of the overall mission, because, otherwise, radar devices on the ground and in Iraqi aircraft would be able to detect the positions of Allied planes. And this would make it easier for Iraqi antiaircraft guns and missiles to shoot down the invading planes.

For these reasons, Allied jets carrying sophisticated antiradar equipment led the way into Iraqi territory. In the first twenty minutes of the attack, these planes jammed Iraqi radar signals, creating static on radar screens. Meanwhile, other high-tech jets fired missiles that homed in on and obliterated Iraqi radar installations. In a scenario unprecedented and seemingly phenomenal by the standards of previous wars, in less than an hour all of Iraq's ground-based radar systems and most Iraqi warplanes were radar "blind." This rendered the Iraqis incapable of detecting or defending against the huge, lethal Allied air armada then entering Iraq. A few Iraqi pilots made visual contact with Allied warplanes and, to their credit, tried to fight the intruders, but these Iraqi planes were shot down immediately, and minutes later the rest of Saddam's air force turned and fled northward.

CNN Scoops the Other Networks

For decades, the three major American television networks—ABC, CBS, and NBC—had dominated the reporting of U.S. and world news events. But that situation changed dramatically on the evening of January 16, 1991, when U.S. warplanes began their massive assault on Iraq. CNN, the Cable News Network, which broadcasts news twenty-four hours a day, gathered a majority of the huge American viewing audience. As U.S. warplanes bombed Baghdad, CNN reporters Bernard Shaw, John Holliman, and Peter Arnett provided electrifying live reports from an Iraqi hotel room. Because they were the only newspeople who managed to continue broadcasting after the bombing began, CNN won exclusive coverage of the story from the other networks. Although some newspeople humorously refer to January 16, 1991, as "the night the networks died," ABC, CBS, and NBC also provided excellent coverage of the war. Often broadcasting live, the four networks brought many of the incidents of the conflict directly into people's homes in stunning detail. Never before had ordinary citizens anywhere in the world been able to watch the dramatic, startling, and disturbing events of a war unfold before their eyes.

American F-16 fighter bombers speed toward Iraqi targets during the largest air assault in history.

In fact, thereafter the Iraqi air force played almost no part at all in defending its country. As to the reasons for this, it was not that Iraq lacked sufficient planes, for it had hundreds of fighters, many of them modern and very capable French-built Mirage F-1s; nor were the pilots all cowards afraid to engage the enemy. Rather, the answer appears to lie in a lack of training and preparedness, as explained by Lawrence Freedman:

> In the period before the onset of hostilities, at most 200 sorties a day were flown by all types of Iraqi aircraft, less than a quarter of its potential, and on the eve of hostilities hardly any were being flown at all. This may have represented a husbanding [saving] of resources, as a result of the embargo, but it ensured that the pilots were poorly trained for such tasks as air-to-air refueling and night flying. Within twenty-four hours of the outbreak of hostilities, Iraqi sorties had plunged from around 100 . . . to some 40 a day; by the end of the first week of fighting there were hardly any Iraqi aircraft in the air. On 24 January three Iraqi aircraft attempted to mount a . . . missile attack against coalition shipping. Two were shot down by a Saudi F-15. From that point, the Iraqi Air Force effectively stood down completely and concentrated on escape.[48]

Air Strikes Hammer Iraq

With most of Iraq's radar warning system crippled and the Iraqi air force on the run, Allied bombers and attack planes were free to attack their targets without fear of being shot down. American F-117A Stealth bombers streaked out of the sky and annihilated Iraqi communications facilities, chemical plants, and nuclear research labs. British Tornado jets swooped low over Iraqi airfields, destroying hangars and creating wide craters on runways to make them useless. Meanwhile, American warships in the Persian Gulf launched more than one hundred Tomahawk cruise missiles equipped with special computerized cameras. These devices were preprogrammed with detailed maps of Iraqi territory, and with deadly accuracy they found and destroyed Iraqi missile sites, oil refineries, and power stations.

In the first few hours of the assault, dozens of Allied warplanes converged on Baghdad, striking the defense ministry, the center for Iraqi war efforts, as well as the presidential palace and the airport. Hundreds of Iraqi antiaircraft guns, many of them located atop office buildings, opened fire on the attackers. But these guns were

Allied Antiradar Weapons

Since its invention in World War II, radar has been an effective way to detect incoming enemy aircraft. A radar antenna sends out invisible radar beams that bounce off the planes and return to a receiver, where a radar operator views the images on a screen. At the outset of the Gulf War, the Iraqis had an extensive network of radar facilities, allowing them to detect enemy planes entering their territory. But they were totally unprepared for the array of sophisticated antiradar weapons possessed by the Allies. First, the United States unleashed its Stealth bombers, which are nearly invisible to radar. The Allies also used U.S.-made Electronic Counter-Measures devices (ECMs). Attached to the U.S. Navy's EA-6B jets, the ECMs detect enemy radar beams and use computers to identify their exact makeup; then, in a split second, the computer sends out a beam of "white noise," a type of static that jams and blinds the enemy's radar. The U.S.-made High-Speed Anti-Radiation Missiles (HARMS), another type of weapon, are high-tech devices that destroy enemy radar installations. Fired from F-4G Wild Weasel Jets, the HARMS home in on the radar beams themselves, reaching and annihilating the antennas.

The F-117A Stealth bomber, one of the most effective and deadly antiradar weapons in the U.S. arsenal.

almost completely useless against the Allied planes, which flew too high and too fast for the bullets to reach them. Like a gigantic fireworks display, the glittering trails of the Iraqi bullets danced in the night sky, while the light from exploding bombs and spreading ground fires illuminated the streets of the Iraqi capital in an eerie glow. Describing the incredible scene from a Baghdad hotel room, CNN reporter Bernard Shaw exclaimed, "Clearly I've never been there, but it feels like we are at the center of Hell!"[49] As Shaw and his companions watched, terrified Iraqi citizens scrambled into air raid shelters or tried to flee the city.

While Allied planes bombed Baghdad, U.S. Apache attack helicopters prowled the deserts of Kuwait. In the darkness, the helicopters used advanced lasers to locate Iraqi troops, bunkers, and tanks and, locking onto their targets, the Apaches blasted away with powerful rockets. At the same time, farther north, huge American B-52 bombers rained tons of explosives on underground bunkers housing members of Saddam's elite Republican Guards.

Overall, during the first eventful day of Operation Desert Storm, the massive Allied air attack took a devastating toll on Iraqi industrial and military facilities. In the first fourteen hours of combat, Allied forces flew more than one thousand sorties (missions, each mission being a single attack-run by one plane) against Iraqi targets, destroying hundreds of buildings and dozens of tanks and other vehicles. According to U.S. military sources, the Allies pounded Iraq with more than twenty-two hundred tons of explosives in the first twenty-four hours of the air assault alone. At the end of that first day,

Iraqi anti-aircraft fire creates a veritable fireworks display during the Allied bombing of Baghdad on January 18, 1991.

with the exception of some ineffective anti-aircraft fire, the Iraqi military still had not managed to mount a counterattack.

Saddam Strikes Back

In a radio broadcast on January 17, one day after the Allied offensive had begun, Saddam Hussein finally responded to the attack on his country. However, it was not a military response, since the Iraqi army continued to offer little or no resistance to the Allied air assault. Instead, Saddam waged a war of words and threats. He called on his countrymen to fight back against the invaders, announcing that the "mother of all battles" had begun and angrily branding President Bush "the Satan of the White House." Saddam also called on all Arabs to rise up against Iraq's enemies. Attempting to incite incidents of international terrorism, he pleaded, "Let the aggressors' interests be set on fire, and let them be hunted down wherever they may be in every corner of the world!" Saddam demanded that Arabs attack the "facilities, symbols, and figures" of the United States and its allies. "The time has come," he said, "to crush the enemy and erase the disgrace."[50] But these pleas and demands apparently went unheeded. In the days that followed, no Arab terrorist attacks were reported in the Middle East or elsewhere in the world.

It was on January 18, 1991, that Saddam finally launched a military counteroffensive, but not against Allied forces. Instead, following through on his threat to strike out at Israel, he ordered a missile attack against

Deadly Cruise Missiles

The Tomahawk cruise missile is one of the most accurate and effective weapons in the high-tech arsenal of the United States. The twenty-foot-long missile has a range of up to fifteen hundred miles and carries a one-thousand-pound warhead, enough explosives to destroy a factory, bridge, or nearly any conventional military target. (Some cruise missiles carry nuclear warheads, but these were not shipped to the Persian Gulf.) The Tomahawk missile is launched from a ship or submarine by a booster rocket. After twelve seconds, a rocket engine on board the missile ignites and powers the weapon. As the missile nears the shore, it "noses down," or flies near ground level, to escape enemy radar detection. After it reaches the land, a computer guidance system called TERCOM activates. The computer has been programmed with maps and satellite photos of both the terrain below and the target itself. An onboard camera scans the ground and compares what it sees with the images stored in the programmed memory, and if the two images do not match, the computer calculates course adjustments. As the weapon nears the target, the computer recognizes it and orders the missile to home in for the kill.

A U.S. destroyer fires one of its lethal Tomahawk cruise missiles during the opening salvo against Saddam's forces.

the Israelis at about 2:00 A.M. Detecting the incoming "Scud" missiles, Israeli defense systems sounded warning sirens. Saddam had warned months before that he would "burn half" of Israel with chemical weapons, and the Israelis were prepared for a poison gas attack. Many Israeli citizens immediately donned gas masks, which their government had distributed in the weeks leading up to the U.N. deadline.

People in the United States and other countries tensely watched live broadcasts of the Israelis waiting for the missiles to fall. Suddenly, about twenty minutes after the missile alert had begun, eight Scuds roared out of the early morning darkness. Two smashed into Israel's largest city, Tel Aviv, three struck the port city of Haifa, and the remaining three landed in open fields. Ambulances, fire fighters, and military personnel that rushed to the impact sites found a great deal of property damage, but thankfully few casualties, for the highly inaccurate Scuds had struck randomly, causing no fatalities and only fifteen injuries.

This attack on Israel generated cries of outrage from people around the world. They pointed out first that Israel was not a member of the Allied coalition, second that it had clearly not provoked the assault, and third that the Iraqis were striking at civilian rather than military targets, a clear violation of international law. Israelis who were interviewed on camera called Saddam a barbarian, a madman, and a coward.

One of Saddam's infamous Scud missiles rests on its launcher (above); the photo at right shows damage done to an Israeli neighborhood by a Scud.

And millions of people around the world heartily agreed. Yet there still existed a small number of Arabs, mainly Jordanians, Syrians, and Palestinians, who applauded Saddam's missile attack on Israel. People in Damascus, Syria, danced in the streets, and a Palestinian woman summed up the feelings of her neighbors when she said, "Let them give Israelis a taste of what they have been inflicting on us for years."[51]

Because Israel is known for its swift and decisive counterattacks, the peoples of many nations were surprised and relieved when Israel did not immediately retaliate against the Iraqis. The primary reason for the Israelis' unusual show of restraint was a request from President Bush. Even as the Scuds were falling on Israel, Bush pleaded with the country's leaders not to strike back, pointing out that an Israeli attack on Iraq would likely enrage all Arabs and that the Saudis and Egyptians might then abandon the Allied operation. This was probably an exaggeration, for the Egyptian ambassador made it clear that his nation would continue to be a part of the Allied coalition even if Israel did retaliate. "Our position is very solid," he declared. "We are part of the coalition [come what may]."[52] Still, American officials felt that it was best not to take any chance of angering their Arab allies. Trying to calm the Israelis, Bush offered to retaliate *for* them by hunting down and destroying the Scud launchers in western Iraq.

Even though they were reluctant to stand by and do nothing while their country was attacked, the Israelis decided not to retaliate at all. This decision was partly in response to pleas from the United States and other Western nations. But Israeli leaders also hoped to send a signal to all Arabs that Israel wanted peace; they hoped that their restraint in the face of Saddam's outrage might lead to better Arab-Israeli relations in the future.

Desperate and Irrational Acts

While launching missiles against Israel, the Iraqis also attacked Saudi Arabia. But just as they had been in Israel, their efforts were random, uncoordinated, and largely ineffective. Allied military commanders believed that Saddam was desperately trying to show the world that he could fight back. But it was clear that he had no overall plan of any consequence or effectiveness. Also, his air force had already been eliminated from the war, and most of his tanks were hidden in desert bunkers to avoid Allied bombers. Therefore, Saddam's only available major offensive weapons were a few Scud missiles and some large artillery guns scattered across southern Iraq and Kuwait.

In their attempts to utilize these weapons, the Iraqis first fired some of their artillery, but most of the shells fell harmlessly into the Saudi desert. Their only direct hit was on the Saudi oil facility near Kafji, on the gulf coast, sections of which exploded and caught fire, sending an ominous plume of black smoke skyward. But the plant was not destroyed and the attack had no effect whatsoever on the Allied

General "Stormin" Norman Schwarzkopf

Norman Schwarzkopf, commander of the coalition forces of Operations Desert Shield and Desert Storm, attended West Point Military Academy in the 1950s. He later served two tours of duty as a junior officer in the Vietnam War. It was there that he picked up the nickname "Stormin Norman," which he claims to hate. He prefers what most of his staff members call him—"the bear." Schwarzkopf's military colleagues say that he is a good soldier who knows how to weigh a situation and get a job done. They credit him with putting together just the right blend of armor, artillery, and airpower in the Gulf War operations. Military experts say he did an excellent job of coordinating the armed forces of the many countries in the Allied coalition, and former marine commandant P. X. Kelley called Schwarzkopf "a superb strategist, a brilliant tactician [goal achiever], tough as nails, and a real troop handler."

General Norman Schwarzkopf, seen here engaging in some friendly banter with some of his troops, won praise for his coordination of Allied forces in the war.

offensive. A few hours later, an Iraqi Scud missile homed in on the Allied air base at Dhahran. Moments before impact, U.S. forces fired a radar-guided Patriot antimissile missile, destroying the Scud in midair, and as the explosion lit up the night sky Allied troops cheered and applauded.

This was the first time that the Patriots had been used in war, and they seemed to prove effective against incoming missiles in the first days of the conflict. Each Patriot missile station consisted of a launcher equipped with four missiles and a mobile radar trailer. After an enemy Scud was launched, the Patriot system's radar tracked the flight of the Scud and then fired an antimissile at it. An advanced guidance system inside the Patriot missile exchanged information with the computers in the radar trailer, allowing the Patriot to home in on the incoming Scud. Finally, as the two weapons neared each other, the Patriot exploded into a shower of lethal metal fragments that destroyed the Scud. After the Patriot's initial success at Dhahran, U.S. commanders decided to ship several Patriot units to Israel to help defend against further Scud attacks on that country. Israeli officials welcomed the missiles, since more Iraqi Scuds fell on Israel on January 19, while the Patriots were being set up. Once again, there was extensive property damage but few casualties. During the next several days, while the Israelis trained to use the Patriots, American technicians operated the missiles.

Saddam continued with these largely ineffective Scud missile attacks out of necessity. Without his air force, and faced with Allied planes firing relentlessly at military targets across his country, he was unable to mount a standard counterattack using planes and tanks. For this reason, Saddam followed up the Scud attacks with other desperate and unconventional tactics. On January 23, for example, the Iraqis began releasing oil from their storage tanks directly into the gulf, creating a black tide that, at the rate of more than 4 million

Two U.S. Patriot missiles light up the skyline of Saudi Arabia's capital city. Seconds after this photo was taken, one of these Patriots destroyed an incoming Iraqi Scud missile.

gallons a day, expanded southward, killing thousands of birds and other animals. U.S. officials called the deliberate oil spill "sick," "irrational," and an act of "environmental terrorism." They theorized that Saddam had released the oil to clog up and close down a Saudi plant that converted seawater into freshwater. Meeting this emergency, Saudi and American engineers quickly erected barriers around the facility, and thanks to their efforts the oil failed to damage the plant's machines.

The Doomed Assault on Kafji

On January 29, 1991, Iraqi forces sped over the border into Saudi Arabia, crossed six miles of desert, and seized control of the small, deserted town of Kafji. U.S. military experts guessed that Saddam was trying to impress Middle Eastern Arabs by launching a ground attack, however pathetic, on the Saudis. But the Allies were perplexed that the Iraqis had entered enemy territory without the standard protection of fighter planes. Former U.S. army colonel David H. Hackworth remarked, "For Iraq to send in armor without air cover. . . was suicidal. . . . It was an operation doomed from the start." It appeared, therefore, that Saddam was willing to send his men to almost certain death in an attempt to bolster his own image. In any case, Allied forces quickly surrounded and attacked Kafji, and after holding the town for only thirty-six hours, most of the Iraqi occupiers turned and fled toward their border. They left behind 30 dead and 429 of their comrades, who, exhausted and frightened, wasted no time in surrendering.

Another ineffective and seemingly irrational Iraqi maneuver occurred a few days later. On January 29, several thousand Iraqi troops suddenly crossed the border into Saudi Arabia and occupied the abandoned town of Kafji, on the gulf shore. This move made no sense from a military standpoint because the town had no strategic significance; U.S. military experts suggested that Saddam was desperately trying to show his Arab supporters that his army could go on the offensive. But that so-called offensive was short-lived, for Allied forces instantly surrounded and shelled the Iraqis in Kafji. Then Saudi soldiers moved into the town, inflicting heavy casualties and capturing nearly five hundred Iraqis. Western military experts and news analysts called the Iraqi attack on Kafji "suicidal," "senseless," and a "humiliating defeat."

Countdown to the Ground Attack

Meanwhile, Allied bombing missions against Iraq continued at the rate of thousands per day. Allied warplanes destroyed bridges, airfields, and military centers, and Iraq's two operating nuclear power plants were leveled. By early February 1991, the 4.5 million people of Baghdad had almost no electricity or running water. Hundreds of Iraqi tanks and trucks had become charred, twisted hulks littering the desert, and most of the country's military and industrial facilities lay in ruins. In addition, tens of thousands of Iraqi military personnel had been killed, while Allied fatalities still numbered fewer than one hundred.

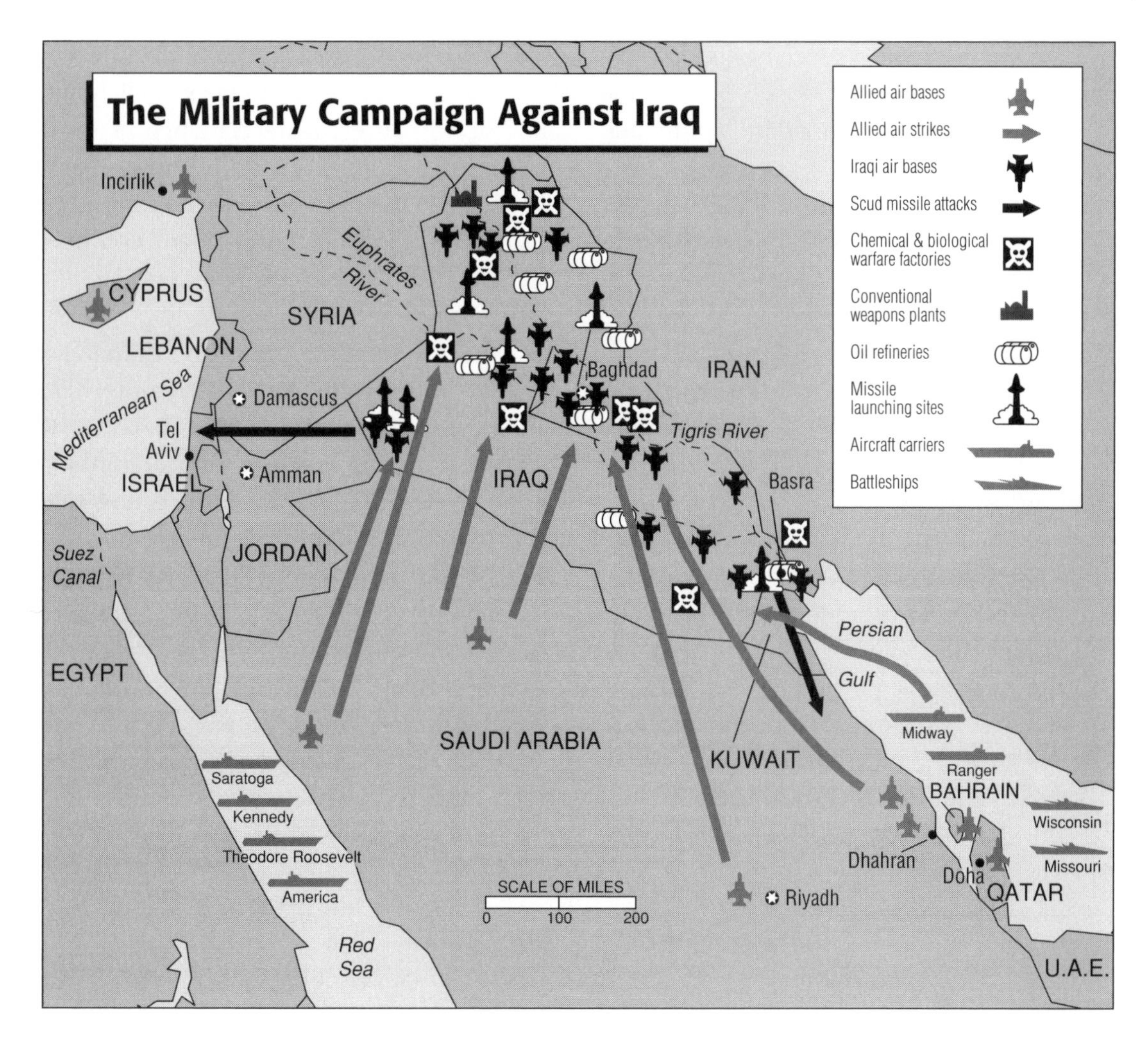

Despite this widespread destruction and misery the air war had brought to his country, Saddam stubbornly refused to order his forces out of Kuwait. In fact, he only continued to respond with irrational, outrageous, and/or self-defeating maneuvers such as destroying Kuwaiti oil wells and other oil facilities, acts that belied his earlier proud claims that he was trying to help the Kuwaitis. As President Bush saw it, such acts constituted simply more nails in the coffin Saddam was constructing for himself. On February 22, Bush delivered a dramatic public warning to the Iraqi dictator, saying that Saddam had to begin withdrawing from Kuwait by noon on February 23 or face a devastating ground assault by Allied forces. "The United States and its coalition allies," Bush said, are committed to enforcing the United Nations resolutions that call for Saddam Hussein to immediately and unconditionally leave Kuwait. . . . We learned this morning that Saddam had now launched a scorched earth policy against Kuwait, anticipating perhaps that he will be forced to leave. He is wantonly setting fire to and destroying the oil wells, the oil tanks, the export terminals, and other installations of that small country. Indeed, they are destroying the entire oil production system of Kuwait. . . . [After] discussing it with my senior advisors . . . I have decided that the time has come to make public with specificity just exactly what is required of Iraq if ground war is to be avoided. Most important, the coalition will give Saddam Hussein until noon [EST] Saturday [February 23, 1991] to do what he must do—begin his immediate and unconditional withdrawal from Kuwait. We must hear publicly and authoritatively his acceptance of these terms. . . . [Otherwise] he risks subjecting the Iraqi people to further hardship unless the Iraqi government complies fully with [these] terms.[53]

Having heard the American ultimatum, people around the world once more held their breath. Some remembered the tough, ominous words of the top-ranking U.S. general, Colin Powell, who had told reporters in January how the Allies would defeat the Iraqi army. "First," said Powell calmly and methodically, "we're going to cut it off [from its supply lines], then we're going to kill it."[54] After weeks of devastating bombing, the Iraqis in Kuwait were, as Powell had predicted, cut off and isolated. Now, apparently, it was time for the Allies to move in for the kill.

☆ Chapter 6 ☆

The Lightning Allied Ground Offensive

The ground attack by Allied troops against Iraq, dubbed "Desert Saber," began at 8:00 P.M. on February 23, 1991, just as President Bush warned that it would. He announced the beginning of the devastating assault two hours later, saying that Iraq had not met the Allied demand to leave Kuwait. Bush explained that he had ordered General Schwarzkopf "to use all forces available, including ground forces, to eject the Iraqi army from Kuwait."[55]

Allied Forces Sweep into Iraq

The overall plan of the Allied attack was to move troops northward into southeastern Iraq and cut off Kuwait from the rest of Iraq. Then the Allies would concentrate on defeating Iraqi forces in Kuwait. The assault relied partly on deception. For weeks preceding the attack, the Allied commanders had kept most of their forces massed in the Saudi desert south of Kuwait, leading the Iraqis to believe that the main thrust of an Allied attack would push northward into Kuwait. But at the last minute, the Allies suddenly shifted most of their troops and tanks toward the west, south of Iraq. The Iraqis were not aware of these changes, mainly because

Allied tanks roll onto Iraqi soil at the start of operation "Desert Saber."

they did not have spotter planes to keep them informed of enemy troop movements. General Schwarzkopf also stationed eighteen thousand U.S. Marines in plain sight in the Persian Gulf near the Kuwaiti coast. Suspecting from this that there would be an amphibious assault (an attack over water), the Iraqis pulled thousands of troops out of the desert and placed them near the coast.

Thus, the Iraqis were taken almost completely by surprise when the bulk of the Allied forces swept northward into Iraq. It was in southeastern Iraq, near the Kuwaiti border, that the Republican Guards had constructed hundreds of underground concrete bunkers. Saddam Hussein had been holding these, his best troops, in reserve. If an Allied ground offensive swept northward through Kuwait, he apparently reasoned, the Republican Guards would keep the enemy from entering Iraq. Now, however, unbeknownst to either Saddam or the guards, thousands of American tanks and other armored vehicles, accompanied by tens of thousands of American and British troops, sped through the desert. Within a mere few hours, they penetrated deeply into Iraq and moved toward the rear of the heavily armored guard positions.

At the same time, farther to the west, hundreds of American helicopters and French troops streaked across southern and central Iraq. They quickly established well-guarded supply bases in the desert, then hurried north to the Euphrates River, where they stood ready to stop a possible Iraqi retreat. These deft moves completely cut off Kuwait and southeastern Iraq from the rest of Iraq so that Saddam's armies in and near Kuwait were trapped.

The Assault on Kuwait

While Allied troops entered Iraq, a combined force of Americans, Saudis, Egyptians, and Syrians launched a lightning assault into southern Kuwait. Hundreds of tanks rolled across the border and opened fire on Iraqi desert positions. Behind them came more than fifty thousand Allied soldiers, who remained ready to throw on their gas masks and chemical protection gear at a moment's notice. But the Iraqi chemical attack many had feared did not materialize. In fact, to the surprise of Allied commanders and soldiers, there was little resistance of any kind from Iraqi troops in southern Kuwait.

The reasons for the weakness of these Iraqi positions soon became clear. Most of the Iraqis in the desert along the Kuwaiti-Saudi border had already been battered into submission by weeks of Allied bombing raids, as hour after hour, day after day, the massive air assaults had pounded the area. Waves of huge U.S. B-52 bombers had glided low and released their deadly cargoes of explosives on the Iraqi bunkers and trenches, reducing tanks, trucks, and other objects above ground into charred masses of twisted metal. For the Iraqi soldiers crowded inside the dark, dusty underground bunkers, it had seemed like a nightmare that would never end. With

Several Iraqis lie dead near the shattered hulk of one of their tanks, casualties of the continuing, massive Allied assault.

each new explosion, the ground had heaved to and fro, covering everything with showers of sand and debris. The deafening blasts had made it nearly impossible to sleep or even to think clearly, and each time a bunker had received a direct hit, dozens of soldiers had died instantly, their bodies torn to shreds by the force of the impact. Even more frightening, every hour or so the bombing would cause a cavern or bunker to collapse, burying its occupants alive. There was little food or water, for the Allied bombing campaign had cut off most supply lines. So there was also little news from the outside world, which meant that most of the Iraqi troops caught in this relentless rain of explosives had received no reports about the events of the war. The fact was that, after weeks of what seemed like a living hell, many of these men no longer cared who was winning the conflict; all they wanted to do was to get out of these holes of misery and death and go home.

It was not surprising, then, that the majority of these weary, frightened, and starving Iraqis chose surrender rather than certain death, the obvious outcome if they tried to resist the huge army at their doorstep. Accordingly, as the Allies approached, white flags popped up from the bunkers and trenches all along the Iraqi defensive lines. In all, more than five thousand Iraqi soldiers surrendered in the first twenty-four hours of the ground war alone, and thousands more gave up in each succeeding hour. Iraqi officers had told these men that the Americans were barbarians who would torture and shoot them on the spot. So many Iraqis crawled on their knees in a heart-rending and unnecessary display of submission, crying openly and begging for their lives. They grabbed and kissed the hands of the astonished American GIs, who could only look on with pity at their defeated and bedraggled enemies.

Allied troop transports barrel into Kuwait in preparation for liberating the tiny country from Saddam's grasp.

Rampage and Massacre

With so little Iraqi resistance in southern Kuwait, the way was clear for an Allied push toward Kuwait's capital. Tens of thousands of Allied troops, spearheaded by American, Saudi, and Kuwaiti forces, moved northward, as tanks of the American Tiger Brigade raced toward the western flank of the city to cut off any Iraqis trying to escape. Aware that the Allies were approaching, frightened Iraqi troops in Kuwait City realized that they would have to leave. But for reasons unknown, they first went on a rampage, burning many houses and businesses, raping Kuwaiti women, and looting homes and stores. One Kuwaiti witness later recalled that the marauding Iraqis took televisions, radios, groceries, and even dog food. Thinking that the Allies would take at least a day or two to reach the city, the Iraqis continued their looting and destruction for many hours. They then loaded their booty into cars, trucks, school buses, and any other vehicles they could find. Their plan was obviously to escape along Kuwait's northern six-lane route, Highway 80, which led from Kuwait City to the southern Iraqi city of Basra.

But the Iraqi plunderers, having badly misjudged the speed of the onrushing Allies, had waited too long and thereby sealed their own fate. They were still loading their vehicles when they caught sight of a long line of Tiger Brigade tanks approaching the city, destroying any moving vehicles in their path. In a wild panic, the Iraqis jumped into their vehicles and made a mad dash for the highway. But so many thousands tried to escape at once, a massive traffic jam formed. In the early morning hours of February 26, the U.S. tanks came within range of this miles-long Iraqi column and opened fire; at the same time, a U.S. military officer later reported, U.S.

planes were given "the word to work over the entire area, to find anything [having to do with the Iraqis] that was moving and take it out."[56] For some forty hours, the Iraqi column was pounded, smashed, and burned in a terrifying massacre that later observers nicknamed the "highway to hell." According to *Newsweek* journalist Tony Clifton, who rode aboard one of the American tanks,

> We got there just before dusk and essentially shot up the front of this column. The group of vehicles we hit included petrol [gasoline] tankers and tanks, so the tanks exploded in these great fountains of white flame from the ammunition. . . . You could see the little figures of soldiers coming out with their hands up. It really looked like a medieval hell—the hell you see in [paintings by the noted artist of the grotesque, Hieronymus] Bosch, because of the great red flames and then these weird little contorted figures [of burning men].[57]

This photo shows only a small portion of the devastation created by Allied bombers and troops on the so-called "highway to hell."

The next morning, Clifton and other Americans inspected the highway, which had been transformed into a virtual graveyard of corpses and gutted vehicles. "As we drove slowly through the wreckage," Clifton remembered,

> [we] splashed through great pools of bloody water. We passed dead soldiers lying as if resting, without a mark on them. We found others cut up so badly, a pair of legs in its trousers would be 50 yards from the top half of the body. . . . Most grotesque of all was the charred corpse of an Iraqi tank crewman, his blackened arms stretched upward in a sort of supplication [prayer].[58]

Kuwait City Liberated

Meanwhile, at nearby Kuwait City airport, Iraqi soldiers attempted to repulse the invading Allies. U.S. Marines poured into the airport, quickly encircled the Iraqis, and then closed in as if tightening a noose. Many Iraqis died as they ran from one building to another seeking cover, and eventually, seeing that their situation was hopeless, the surviving Iraqi defenders gave up. In the next few hours, other Iraqis tried to escape through the desert, but Allied forces killed or captured them. In all, thousands of Iraqis died in the vicinity of Kuwait City, and many thousands more were wounded or captured. By contrast, in the three days of fighting to retake the capital and airport, the Americans counted just five dead and forty-eight wounded; other Allied casualties were also light. In other parts of Kuwait, those Iraqis who could make good their escape toward Iraq's border did so as fast as possible. Poking fun at Saddam's earlier reference to the "mother of all battles," U.S. defense secretary Dick Cheney quipped, "The Iraqi forces are conducting the mother of all retreats."[59]

On February 27, less than four days after the ground offensive began, Allied forces moved into Kuwait City, now largely free of Iraqi soldiers. Out of courtesy, the Americans waited on the outskirts of the city, allowing Kuwaiti and other Arab forces to go in first and officially reclaim the capital. When the Americans entered a few

Jubilant Kuwaiti troops ride an Allied tank into Kuwait City during their country's liberation.

Overly Anxious to Surrender

Starving and exhausted after weeks of Allied bombing raids, tens of thousands of Iraqi soldiers in southern Kuwait surrendered during the one-hundred-hour ground war. Many Iraqis were so anxious to surrender that they gave themselves up to any foreigners they encountered. On February 28, 1991, for example, a dozen Iraqi soldiers approached an Italian news crew covering the war in the desert. The Iraqis waved white flags and held their hands in the air, and when it became clear that the Italians were not going to shoot them, the smiling Iraqis chanted such phrases as "We salute Italy!" and "God smile on Italy!" in broken Italian. The journalists then gave their prisoners crackers and water, the first meal many of the Iraqis had enjoyed in days. Repeatedly cursing Saddam Hussein, the prisoners explained how they had fled their trenches and walked eighteen miles intending to surrender. About an hour later, fourteen more Iraqis surrendered to the same astounded Italian crew. Later that day, the journalists wished their prisoners good luck as they handed them over to members of the Red Cross. In all, more than a hundred Iraqis gave themselves up to news crews from various nations.

Allied soldiers guard a column of captured Iraqi troops. Thousands of Iraqis surrendered during the war.

hours later, thousands of jubilant Kuwaitis greeted them, some leaping up onto tanks and trucks and kissing the American soldiers. Shouting their thanks to President Bush and other Allied leaders, many Kuwaitis screamed, "Down with Saddam!" and burned large paintings of the dictator that the Iraqis had earlier erected in city squares. Simultaneously, people everywhere fired rifles into the air to celebrate the freeing of the city.

Saddam was not "down" yet, despite the many recent Iraqi reverses. Apparently desperate to save face, Saddam, throughout the last days of the Allied air offensive and first days of the ground attack, had ranted, raved, and released one piece of ludicrous propaganda after another. Even as Kuwait was slipping through his fingers, he claimed that it was rightfully a part of Iraq; that the members of the Allied coalition were evil aggressors that sooner or later would be destroyed by God and righteous Arabs; and that the war would continue, since the Iraqis were clearly winning! Practically no one took this bluster seriously, of course, since it was obvious to even the most pro-Iraqi observer that Iraq was losing the war. Moreover, there seemed little chance that Saddam would suddenly produce some military miracle and repulse the Allies, for it had already been demonstrated repeatedly that the Iraqi dictator and his top advisers had little or no skill in conducting military strategy and logistics. In this regard, when asked, on February 27, the same day the Allies liberated Kuwait City, what he thought of his opponent's abilities as a military man, General Schwarzkopf replied with a smirk:

> As far as Saddam Hussein being a great military strategist, he is neither a strategist, nor is he schooled in the operational arts, nor is he a tactician, nor is he a general, nor is he a soldier. Other than that, he's a great military man, I want you to know that.[60]

The Allies Crush Iraq's Army

Although Kuwait City had been liberated, the war was not yet over. The large force of Republican Guards in southeastern Iraq was still very much intact, and the Allies had to eliminate this threat before Kuwait would be safe from Iraqi attack. This task was accomplished in what became the largest tank battle fought since World War II. On February 27, 1991, while American and Arab forces were liberating Kuwait City, the massive U.S. Army Seventh Corps closed in on the Republican Guards. The Seventh's more than one thousand tanks and armored carriers and tens of thousands of men had traveled nearly two hundred miles in less than three days. This impressive feat was made possible in large part by an enormous, perfectly coordinated supply effort involving thousands of U.S. helicopters and trucks. Each day, they ferried, among other things, 5,000 tons of ammunition, 555,000 gallons of fuel, 300,000 gallons of water, and 80,000 meals into the battle zone.

Unlike their countrymen in southern Kuwait, most of the Republican Guards were ready to put up a stiff fight. The guard forces consisted of more than three hundred tanks and nearly sixty thousand men, most of them battle-hardened in the Iraq-Iran war. Still, like other Iraqi forces in recent weeks, the guards were mightily surprised when the Americans swung around through southern Iraq and approached Iraqi positions from behind.

In the desert, fifteen miles west of Basra, Iraq's second-largest city, the two armies clashed in what can only be described as furious, no-holds-barred combat. First, the American tanks drew up in a miles-long arc around the guard positions and opened fire. The Iraqis then returned fire as best as they could, but they were not nearly as well trained as the Allies in maneuvering large groups of tanks. Also, the Iraqis' aging, Soviet-made T-55 tanks were no match for the more than eight hundred U.S. M-1A1 high-tech tanks that began to close in on them. With deadly precision, advanced laser systems on the M-1A1s locked in on their targets and guided shells

American High-Tech Ground Weapons

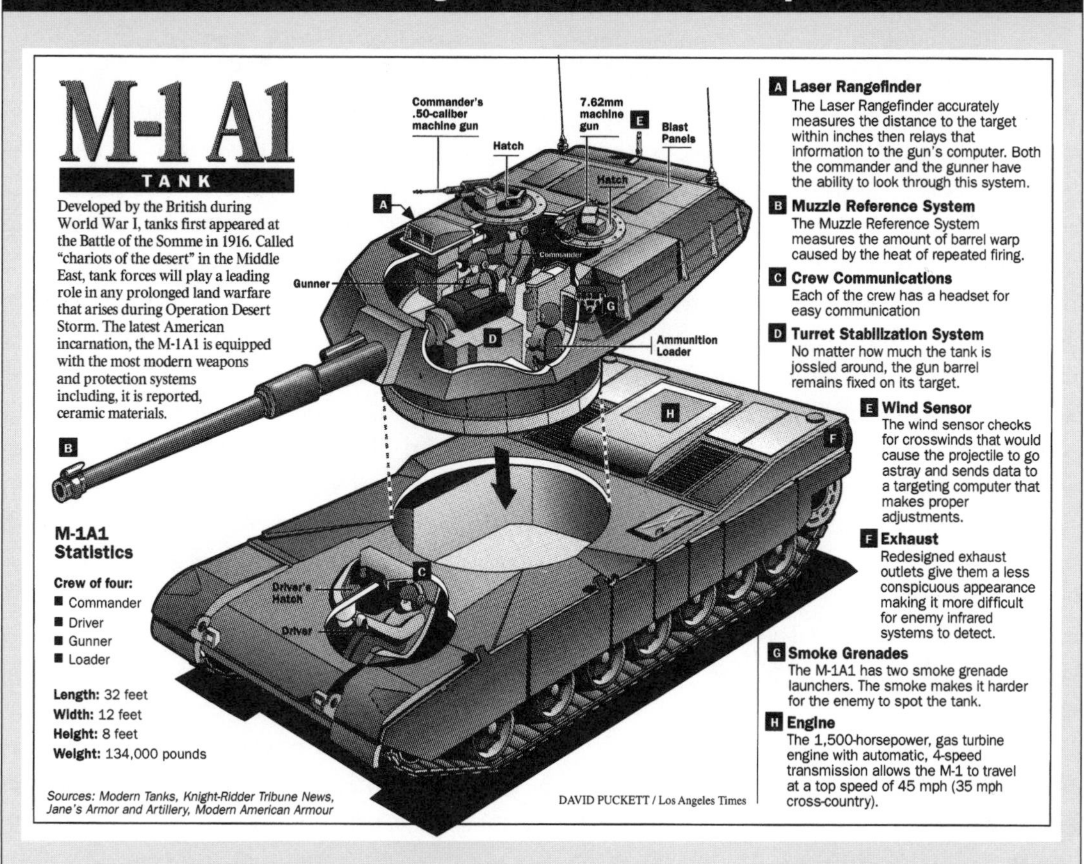

The primary U.S. ground weapon of the Gulf War was the M-1A1 Abrams tank. Called by some military experts "the high-tech tank of all time," the fifty-five-ton M-1A1 fires a special nonnuclear shell called a uranium bolt that can travel up to two miles and penetrate the armor of conventional enemy tanks. By contrast, the shells from most foreign-made tanks cannot penetrate the M-1A1's armor. Each M-1A1, costing $4.4 million to build in 1990, is equipped with an array of advanced devices designed to protect the crew from nuclear, chemical, and biological attacks.

Another effective high-tech ground weapon is the Copperhead, a laser-guided antitank device. Its laser systems provide near-pinpoint accuracy for its powerful shells, which cost $50,000 each. Also in the U.S. arsenal during the Persian Gulf War were the Quick Fix helicopter, designed to jam and confuse enemy radio communications, and the Mobile Subscriber Equipment (MSE), a giant computerized communications system that links more than ten thousand U.S. battle radios at one time.

to direct hits on Iraqi tanks, trucks, and artillery pieces.

At the same time, U.S. Apache helicopters and A-10 attack planes pounded the Iraqis from the air. Under this rain of fire, many of the Iraqi tanks exploded into huge fireballs, sending metal fragments, some weighing tons, flying in every direction. Most of the Republican Guards inside these tanks were instantly burned to death. The few who survived the pounding, their clothes and hair aflame, ran screaming across the sands and directly into lethal hails of U.S. rockets and machine-gun bullets. Meanwhile, more of the guards poured from their bunkers and tried to help their comrades by firing their machine guns at the Allies. But their efforts had little effect on the massive and well-coordinated array of tanks and aircraft that bore down on them.

By the morning of February 28, after more than ten hours of bloody combat, the surviving Republican Guards finally surrendered. Thousands of Iraqis lay dead amid the smashed remains of more than two hundred of their tanks. In comparison, fewer than twenty Americans had died and no U.S. tanks had been destroyed in the fighting. As U.S. troops rounded up the Iraqi prisoners, President Bush announced on television,

> Kuwait is liberated. Iraq's army is defeated. Our military objectives are met. America and the world drew a line in the sand. We declared that the aggression against Kuwait would not stand, and tonight America and the world have kept their word.[61]

Kuwait Devastated

In just one hundred hours, the lightning Allied ground offensive had cut off Kuwait from Iraq, freed the Kuwaiti people, and crushed the Iraqi army. Overall during the forty-three-day war, the Iraqis counted at least 50,000 dead (with some estimates ranging as high as 82,000 dead), another 50,000 or more wounded, and more than 125,000 captured. The combined Allied forces, by contrast, had suffered only 177 killed, 597 wounded, and fewer than 60 taken prisoner. (This does not count another couple of hundred Americans who died in training and routine accidents in the months leading up to the actual outbreak of fighting.) At a briefing held for reporters in Saudi Arabia, General Schwarzkopf gave much of the credit for these low Allied casualty figures and the overwhelming Allied victory to the soldiers who fought in the desert. Calling them "heroes" and their performances under fire "brilliant," he said that "we ought to be very, very proud of them."[62]

But even though the Allied victory was indeed a total one, it was partly overshadowed by the grim specter of the devastation the Iraqi occupiers had wrought on Kuwait and its people. Apparently out of sheer hatred and cruelty, the Iraqis had killed thousands of Kuwaitis and tortured many more. During the months of Iraqi occupation, Kuwait's four major medical centers accu-

American Women in the Gulf

"Mom, if you die over there, I'm coming to rescue you," said Lt. Col. Carolyn Roaf's daughter as they said good-bye. Roaf was on her way with thousands of other American women soldiers to serve in the Persian Gulf. Women have taken part in all U.S. wars, but, as journalist Melinda Beck reports, never "on such a large scale or in such a wide variety of jobs." Of the 2 million people serving in the U.S. armed forces in 1990, 11 percent were women. And women make up 7 percent of U.S. sailors and army gun crews, 10 percent of secret intelligence gatherers, and 35 percent of administrators. In addition, 10 percent of the military's officers are women. In Saudi Arabia, women pilots flew helicopters carrying troops and supplies, and women mechanics maintained tanks and trucks and served as navigators, communications experts, and paratroopers (parachute jumpers).

According to U.S. law, women still cannot take part in actual combat, but commanders no longer remove them from dangerous areas when fighting begins. The dangers faced by women serving in Operation Desert Storm became clear in early February 1991 when U.S. patrols found an abandoned American truck near the Saudi-Kuwaiti border. Two GIs were missing, one of them twenty-year-old Melissa Rathbun-Nealy, from Newaygo, Michigan. Luckily, she was later released along with other American POWs. Despite such danger, women soldiers insist that they should receive no special treatment just because they are women. They say that they are doing their jobs just like the men and are willing to take the same risks. But many Americans still hold on to traditional ideas about protecting women. Explained *Newsweek*'s Tom Morganthau, "The question is how the public will react to seeing women held captive–and possibly tortured–by the enemy. For women in the military, attaining equality may carry a terrible price."

An American woman soldier operates her equipment during the Allied offensive.

mulated the corpses of dozens of Kuwaitis who had been mutilated by Iraqi soldiers; there were bodies with ax wounds, for instance, as well as some with ears cut off, eyes gouged out, intestines inflated with air, and skulls sawed in half, to name only a few of the atrocities. The Iraqis also beat thousands of innocent people, raped hundreds of Kuwaiti women, looted stores, burned buildings, and transported truckloads of Kuwaiti property to Iraq. They stole cars, furniture, televisions, kitchen and other appliances, printing presses, street lamps, entire college libraries, and hundreds of museum artifacts, many of which they intended to sell. In addition, they destroyed several hotels and government buildings, including the headquarters of the Kuwaiti parliament. Finally, they trashed the emir's palace, stealing or breaking everything not nailed down and smearing the floors with human excrement.

Some of the many oil wells set ablaze at Saddam's orders burn out of control, darkening Middle Eastern skies.

As if these despicable acts were not enough, the Iraqis continued their ruinous rampage even after the ground war had begun. When they knew that defeat was imminent, they instituted a "scorched earth" policy, the systematic destruction of the things the enemy would find most valuable. In all, teams of Iraqi soldiers set ablaze some 640 of Kuwait's 950 oil wells, unleashing thick columns of black smoke and dust that blotted out the sun, creating twilight at noon across much of Kuwait. These wells continued to burn out of control for many months afterward.

Horrified by this wanton destruction, the Allies issued stern demands, which the Iraqis had to accept in order to bring about a permanent cease-fire. President Bush made it plain that the present halt in the Allied bombing of Iraq might be only temporary. He warned that the Allies could and would resume the war immediately and with punishing effect if the Iraqis did not agree to Allied terms. First and foremost, said Bush, the Iraqis must immediately free all Allied prisoners of war. Allied planes, ships, and ground forces then stood by, on full alert, waiting to see if this initial demand would be met; the proverbial ball was now in the court of the defeated but notoriously unpredictable dictator, Saddam Hussein.

☆ Chapter 7 ☆

More Troubles for Iraq and the Middle East

The Allied coalition, led by U.S. forces, had won an impressive victory over the Iraqi army and liberated Kuwait from Saddam Hussein's grasp. But while this huge and successful mission had solved the immediate problem of Kuwait's earlier seizure, sadly it had not brought permanent peace and stability to the region. For one thing, the Allies had stopped short of a full-scale invasion of Iraq with the goal of toppling Saddam from power. U.S. and other Allied leaders had assumed that once they had crushed the Iraqi dictator's forces and ruined the military and industrial infrastructure of his country, the Iraqi people would do the rest. The hope was that popular local rebellions would topple Saddam's regime and a friendlier, less-dangerous regime would take its place. But this overly optimistic scenario did not play out. At the end of the war, Saddam remained very much intact as Iraq's leader, for though his defeat had badly embarrassed his regime, it had not significantly weakened its hold on Iraq and its people. The result was that in the years ahead he remained a potent threat to his neighbors and a constant thorn in the side of the Allies. And Iraq continued to capture headlines as a source of unrest and trouble for the Middle East and world community at large.

"Aggression is Defeated"

Such a bleak and unwelcome turn of events was certainly the last thing on the minds of the Allies at the close of the Gulf War. For one brief and shining moment, Allied leaders reveled in the immediate euphoria generated by their victory, while millions of people around the world celebrated what was seen as the triumph of the forces of freedom over those of tyranny. In the United States, President Bush's popularity soared. Addressing a televised joint session of Congress on March 6, 1991, he received a thunderous standing ovation after announcing, "Aggression is defeated . . . the war is over." As General Schwarzkopf

Saddam's Continuing Propaganda Campaign

Though the physical war between Iraq and the Western Allies has long been over, Saddam continues to wage a war of propaganda in his own country. His intent is to make it look as though Iraq actually won the war, despite the obvious devastation of the Allied bombing. Part of his approach is visual. Huge paintings and statues of himself are erected each year in Iraqi town squares, most of them depicting him as a victorious leader. One recent example in Baghdad shows him in his army uniform standing atop the flattened faces of Allied leaders, including President Bush, Britain's Margaret Thatcher, and Saudi Arabia's King Fahd. The dictator's regime also tightly controls the press, television news and other programming, school textbooks, and other means by which Iraqis might learn the truth. No foreign TV reports reached Baghdad during the war, for example, and it is strictly forbidden to own a satellite dish in Iraq. This propaganda campaign has worked at least to some degree. An Iraqi man interviewed by an American journalist in 1999 stated flatly, "A big battle was fought between Iraqi tanks and American tanks, and Iraq won." Still, some Iraqis have managed, through secret and illegal means, to learn the truth and have not been fooled by their leader.

A huge statue of Saddam Hussein stands above pieces of U.S. missiles collected by Iraqi citizens.

had done earlier, the president gave credit for the victory to the soldiers. "This victory belongs to them," he declared,

> to the finest fighting force this nation has ever known. We went halfway around the world to do what is moral and just and right. And we fought hard and, with others, we won the war [to lift] the yoke of tyranny and aggression from a small country that many Americans had never even heard of. . . . Thank you guys, thank you very, very much![63]

Bush had put into words what most Americans felt with great pride. The U.S. all-volunteer army of regular and reserve soldiers had proved itself to be a well-coordinated and superior fighting force. When called on to go to war and risk their lives, these men and women had risen to the challenge and performed their jobs efficiently, professionally, and courageously. Years after Vietnam, Americans once more had confidence in their military and pride in their country. Said President Bush at a White House meeting, "By God, we've kicked the Vietnam syndrome [loser image] once and for all!"[64] Evidence of the truth of these words came when U.S. troops began returning home from the Persian Gulf. Everywhere, the soldiers received triumphant heroes' welcomes, in contrast to so many of the Vietnam veterans, who had been either criticized or ignored after they had come home. Excited crowds greeted the Gulf War soldiers as they arrived home on planes and ships. There were parades in their honor all over the nation, and President Bush asked that special celebrations be held for the returning heroes on July 4, 1991.

The jubilant mood in the U.S., which was matched in Britain and other Allied nations, was understandable. Almost everything in the war had gone in the Allies' favor; in particular, many of the dire predictions voiced by diplomats, military experts, and war critics before the war began had never come true. Some had warned, for example, that it would likely be a long conflict, that Saddam would draw the United States and its partners into another costly and draining Vietnam. But the total Allied victory had come in only forty-three days. Others had predicted that Saddam's huge, battle-hardened army would inflict heavy casualties on the Allies, weakening the

Returning American soldiers take part in an enormous victory parade in New York City in March 1991.

spirit and resolve of the Western countries. But to the contrary, most Iraqi troops—ill equipped and supplied, ineptly led, and lacking in morale—had either surrendered or offered only token resistance.

Moreover, other much-feared events had not transpired. Many people had been certain that the Iraqis would use chemical weapons, adding a terrifying dimension to the conflict. But as it happened, Iraqi commanders had held back, fearing that the Allies might respond in kind. And Saddam's dreaded pan-Arab jihad, spearheaded by a worldwide wave of terrorism, had never materialized. According to U.S. officials, many would-be terrorists had concluded that Saddam's was a lost cause or were discouraged by tight security measures instituted around the globe.

In spite of these positive developments, a few people in the United States, including some members of Congress, pointed out that the victory was incomplete because the Allies had failed to remove Saddam from power. This, they said, would make it impossible for the Iraqi people to form a new, more democratic kind of government. (But was this what the Iraqi people as a whole actually wanted? Few Americans seemed to consider this crucial question.) Yet most people in the West were not in the mood to speculate about what might happen as a result of Saddam's continued reign. Surely, went the conventional reasoning, the Iraqi people would not long tolerate a leader who had led them to such a humiliating defeat.

The Fruits of Victory

For the moment at least, because the Allies had been so successful, they were in a position to dictate whatever cease-fire terms they wanted to the Iraqis. General Schwarzkopf set the time and place of a meeting between Allied and Iraqi commanders. On March 3, 1991, a bit less than six days after the fighting had ceased, they met at a captured Iraqi airfield in Safwan, near the Iraqi-Kuwaiti border. The tent in which the meeting took place was surrounded by more than fifty tanks draped in U.S. and British flags. Schwarzkopf made an impressive, theatrical entrance, arriving in a squadron of six Apache attack helicopters, while, by contrast, the two Iraqi generals arrived in open jeeps.

After the two-hour private meeting, attended by high Saudi, British, and French leaders as well as Schwarzkopf and the Iraqis, the American general shook hands with and saluted his Iraqi counterparts. Shortly afterward, Schwarzkopf told reporters that he was "very happy to tell you that we agreed on all matters." The Saudi commander added that the Iraqis had been willing "not only to answer, but to satisfy us in every request we had."[65] The most important term agreed on by these men was the release of Allied prisoners. Accordingly, within three days, as demanded, the Iraqis released all the Allied POWs they held to the Red Cross. Another cease-fire term called for Allied and Iraqi forces to avoid contact, ostensibly to reduce tension between the armies and make potential in-

General Schwarzkopf sits across from Iraqi negotiators at the cease-fire meeting on March 3, 1991.

cidents that might lead to further violence less likely. The agreement also demanded that the Iraqis provide information about the location of their explosive land mines in Kuwait. Without this information, finding and destroying Iraqi land mines would be a random, dangerous process in which many Allied soldiers and Kuwaiti citizens might be killed.

Iraq Torn by Civil Strife

As it turned out, the cease-fire observed between the Iraqis and the Allies did not ensure peace in Iraq. On March 6, 1991, a mere three days after the meeting at Safwan, Iraqi citizens in several southern cities rose in rebellion. The war had significantly weakened Saddam's army and disrupted the government's communications and transportation networks. So those Iraqis who opposed Saddam's dictatorship decided that the time was as ripe as it would ever be to attempt to topple his regime. These rebels were driven in part by the confident feeling that they would not be fighting Saddam alone. Many times during the gulf crisis President Bush had called on the Iraqi people to rise up and overthrow Saddam, and the rebels were now convinced that American troops, who were still in the region, would help them in their struggle.

The rebellion was especially fierce and bloody in the southern city of Basra. There, some regular Iraqi soldiers boldly joined the rebels and fired their tanks into a huge portrait of Saddam as furious street fighting engulfed the city. Rebels stormed the local prison and released the inmates, most of whom had been jailed for opposing the government.

A Kurdish rebel guerrilla fighter proudly displays his automatic weapon.

The unrest quickly spread to other sections of Iraq. In the northern part of the country, most significantly, tens of thousands of ethnic Kurds engaged in guerrilla warfare with Iraqi army units. The Kurds' language and customs are very different from most other Iraqis, and they had been demanding their own homeland for decades. Having rebelled before, the Kurds were familiar with the wrath and tactics of Saddam, who in the 1980s had destroyed some five thousand Kurdish villages, leaving the survivors homeless and starving. In 1988, moreover, he had unleashed chemical weapons on a Kurdish town, killing more than five thousand people and forcing hundreds of thousands of Kurds to flee into Turkey and Iran. Now the remaining Iraqi Kurds believed that their chance had finally come to break free of Saddam's brutal rule.

For more than two weeks, the Kurds and other rebels fought Saddam's troops in many sections of the country. But by late March, the tide had begun to turn in the government's favor, as Iraqi attack helicopters launched devastating raids on crowds of civilians as well as rebel fighters. As crippled rebel forces retreated, they wondered what had happened to American support for the uprising Bush had encouraged. And echoing this theme, some members of the U.S. Congress criticized the president for not helping the rebels after so forcefully encouraging them to revolt. But Bush responded that the U.N.-sponsored goal of the Allies had been to liberate Kuwait, not to get involved in Iraq's internal troubles. To this, rebel leaders retorted that it had been the Gulf War that had sparked the rebellions in the first place; they were risking their lives, they said, to overthrow Saddam as the Americans had urged, yet now, seemingly, the Americans had abandoned them. As the rebels' plight grew worse, a growing number of people in the West began to feel that the U.S. failure to aid them constituted a stain on the otherwise shining Allied victory.

Saddam's Revenge

By late April 1991, Saddam's troops had crushed the rebellions. And the rebels began to pay a heavy price for daring to defy the dictator. As late as the year 2000, nine years after the end of the Gulf War, many bridges and other structures in the city of Basra had not been rebuilt, as they had been in Baghdad and some other parts of Iraq. This was clearly intended as punishment. "One of the biggest factors in Saddam's mentality is revenge," said an Iraqi now living in London. "He will never forgive them [the people of Basra] for revolting."[66]

In the north, meanwhile, in April and May 1991, an estimated 2 million Kurds fled their homes for the mountains of northern Iraq. These refugees, who camped on rough, muddy hillsides with little food and no fresh water, died at the rate of at least a thousand a day. Relief efforts by member countries of the United Nations could not bring enough food and medical supplies fast enough to reduce the severity of the crisis to any significant degree. Meanwhile, American, British, and other Allied troops patrolled some northern towns and tried to get the Kurds to return to their homes. But most of the refugees refused to return for fear of being massacred by Saddam's soldiers after the Allies left.

These are some of the bridges and other structures at Basra that Saddam refused to rebuild in order to punish the city.

When, after many weeks, the Allied patrols did leave, Kurdish leaders met with Saddam Hussein and worked out a temporary cease-fire between rebel and government forces. This cease-fire was supported and enforced by daily flights of U.S. warplanes, which discouraged Iraqi troops from moving northward into Kurdish enclaves. Going a step further to maintain the peace, the United States and Britain established a "no fly zone" over northern Iraq in 1991, warning that Iraqi aircraft must stay out of it or risk being shot down. With these safeguards in place, the Kurds were more or less left alone to govern themselves. In the spring of 1992, the local Kurds held an election that established an assembly, forming the nucleus of the Kurdish Regional Government (KRG), which struggled to administer and provide food and other supplies for its people. This was a difficult task, for the Kurds were not only cut off from the rest of Iraq, they were also the victims of an embargo imposed by Saddam, who refused to ship them even humanitarian aid from Baghdad.

A Continuing Standoff with the Kurds

That Saddam wanted to achieve a further measure of revenge on the defiant Kurds and force them back into the Iraqi fold became evident when he attacked them again in 1996. Iraqi troops swept into the northern town of Arbil on August 31, captured it, and executed on the spot a number of Iraqi rebels who had set up a headquarters there. Soon afterward, Saddam ordered his troops out of the city, having achieved his goal of demonstrating that he could strike at will in the area.

In early September 1996, the U.S. president, Bill Clinton (elected in 1992), responded to the Iraqi move into the Arbil area by launching a batch of cruise missiles at military targets in Iraq. "Our mission has been achieved," Clinton boasted afterward. "Saddam is strategically worse off [than he was before]. . . . He knows that there is a

President Bill Clinton makes a point at a news conference shortly after launching cruise missiles against Iraq.

price to be paid for stepping over the line."[67] However, there were many critics in the U.S. and Middle East who saw the U.S. response as too little, too late, and barely a slap on Saddam's wrist. "The subdued American response gave Saddam Hussein his first big political success since the invasion of Kuwait," explain Middle Eastern news correspondents Patrick and Andrew Cockburn. "He had calculated that the United States would not intervene [in a major way], especially if he withdrew quickly, and he had been right."[68] One American Middle Eastern expert expanded on this view:

> I am ashamed. In the Middle East you either get it done to you, or you do it to someone else. It's a male thing [referring to the traditional custom of male dominance in Arabic society]. We essentially did nothing to Saddam, nothing. We showed weakness. This will be seen in the region as shameful to Mr. Clinton.[69]

(The 1996 U.S. cruise missile attack did not mark the first time that Clinton had bombed Iraq to punish Saddam. In 1993, American agents had uncovered a plan by Iraqi secret security forces to assassinate ex-president George Bush during an upcoming trip to Kuwait. Clinton had responded by launching twenty-three cruise missiles at Iraq's intelligence headquarters in Baghdad.)

The standoff between Saddam and the Kurds continues. And though the Kurds attempt to lead normal lives, out of fear of more attacks from Baghdad they maintain what is in essence an armed camp. This was clearly revealed in a 1999 report filed by Western journalist Mike Edwards, who spent several weeks among the Kurds. "Life is much improved for the Kurds," he says,

> but they are, as ever, disunited and prone to settle disputes with guns. Everyone seemed to have [automatic rifles]. I saw two women at a wedding with rifles slung on their shoulders, and when I looked into the car that would whisk the new couple away, I saw a rifle on the front seat. Some Kurds carried weapons because their families were involved in feuds, others because they were *peshmerga*, warriors. "If something happens suddenly, we are ready," said a *peshmerga*, strolling through a bazaar with his weapon. . . . [The various leading and rival Kurdish political parties] say their goal isn't independence from Iraq but the right to control their own affairs—under a government not run by Saddam Hussein, of course.[70]

The Problem of Saddam's Lethal Weapons

Those who pointed out that the 1993 and 1996 missile strikes against Saddam had not hurt him much in the short run and not at all in the long run became increasingly worried. The longer the Iraqi dictator remained in power, they warned, the more likely it was that he would continue to work

The Danger of Land Mines

In 1999, Western journalist Mike Edwards visited the Kurds in northern Iraq and examined their lives and problems firsthand. One particularly dangerous problem they face, he says, is the existence of large numbers of land mines lingering from the many years of fighting. "Everyone who fought in these mountains—Iraqis, Iranians, Kurds—laid mines," says Edwards in a revealing article for *National Geographic.*

> Millions remain in the earth. In a village of mud and stone, a man showed me his hands. Five digits were missing. He had also lost an eye. "I was trying to clear a field so I could plant," he said. "I saw this thing and I lifted it and. . ." A thin woman standing in a doorway said, "Seventeen people of this village have been killed or hurt by mines.". . . "Clearing the mines could be a matter of life and death for these people . . ." said Graeme Abernathy, who was with me. . . . Graeme led a team of de-miners brought in by the U.N. to teach their hazardous craft to the Kurds. "If you take out one mine, you may save the life of one person," said Roger Sabah, a Kurdish de-miner. "It is not dangerous if you are careful.". . . Standing well away, I watched him work. On his knees he marked off an area measuring about one foot by three feet. He checked for trip wires, trimmed the grass, and gently felt the earth. Finally, he passed a metal detector over the area. Satisfied, he advanced another foot. In a day, he'd cover perhaps ten square yards.

on his pet projects—his weapons of mass destruction. This trepidation came from a disquieting revelation that had emerged in the years immediately following the 1991 Gulf War. This was that most of Saddam's programs and facilities for producing these weapons had not been destroyed in the war. According to the Cockburns,

> Sites known to be associated with the Iraqi nuclear program were given high priority in the bombing plans and were duly pulverized during the air offensive. . . . By the end of the war, the White House and the Pentagon congratulated themselves on having destroyed the bulk of Saddam's nuclear weapons manufacturing potential. In fact, though the bombing had inflicted severe damage, the U.S. high command was being overly optimistic. The [enormous] Iraqi . . . complex at al-Atheer, south of Baghdad, that was the center of the entire nuclear effort, escaped unscathed, its very existence unknown to the Americans. . . . [Moreover] Saddam still had large stocks of chemical ammunition on hand. His main biological-weapons production center at al-Hakam had remained untouched. The enemy did not even know it existed.[71]

When it started to become clear that Saddam was still developing weapons of mass destruction, the United Nations created the so-called Special Commission. It consisted of a team of inspectors to be sent into Iraq, experts from several nations who were trained to recognize and evaluate such advanced weapons programs. At first, Saddam figured he could easily evade the inspectors. "The Special Commission is a temporary measure," he told some of his associates. "We will fool them and we will bribe them and the matter will be over in a few months."[72] But to Saddam's chagrin, the inspectors were not so easily fooled or bribed and ended up staying some seven years and uncovering a great deal of revealing and important information. Typically, the Iraqis followed the same basic pattern in dealing with the inspectors and their discoveries. Regarding biological weapons, for example, first the government denied that it had ever worked on such weapons at all; when the inspectors found proof that it had, the government admitted that it had worked on biological weapons but insisted that it had never actually built any; then, when the inspectors showed proof that this was also a lie, the Iraqis admitted that they had built such weapons but claimed they had halted all production of them in 1991. This, of course, was also a lie.

Increasingly embarrassed and eventually seething with anger, Saddam did everything he could to obstruct the inspectors. In October 1997 he tested the Allies' and U.N.'s resolve by expelling the Americans on the inspection team, which provoked a crisis. For a while, it looked as though President Clinton would bomb Iraq again, this time on a much larger scale than in 1993 or 1996. Fortunately, this move became unnecessary, for in mid-November Saddam backed down, announcing that he would allow the American inspectors to return. The situation did not improve very much, however, as the Iraqis continued to throw up roadblocks to the inspectors. These actions provoked President Clinton to order another limited air strike against Iraq in December 1998, after which the Iraqi government kicked the inspectors out of the country for good.

A Devastated People

President Clinton and other Allied leaders reacted to Saddam's eviction of the weapons inspectors in the only way that they could. This was to promise to sustain the economic sanctions that had been imposed against Iraq before the 1991 Gulf War, a massive embargo that had remained in effect in the years that followed. The American and Allied policy of maintaining these harsh sanctions had been spelled out by an American official in May 1991. "Saddam is discredited," he stated,

> and cannot be redeemed. His leadership will never be accepted by the world community. Therefore, Iraqis will pay the price while he remains in power. All possible sanctions will be maintained until he is gone. . . . Any easing of sanctions will be considered only when there is a new government [in Iraq].[73]

Whether one agrees or disagrees with maintaining the sanctions on Iraq, no one can deny that the combination of these measures with the damage done by U.S. bombing (especially in the 1991 air offensive) has been devastating for that country and its people. Before the war and sanctions, the World Bank had classified Iraq's social and economic level as being equivalent to that of Greece, a moderately advanced Western nation. Afterward, by contrast, a United Nations official remarked that "Iraq has, for some time to come, been relegated to a pre-industrial age."[74] Another U.N. official, Denis Halliday, who did humanitarian work in Iraq in 1997 and 1998, agreed, pointing out, "The infrastructure [of the country] is collapsing and it will take ten to twenty years to restore."[75] He noted, for example, that the electric power system was in most places shattered and beyond repair, with generators so old that no one made spare parts for them any more. Halliday estimated that it would take up to $10 billion to restore Iraq's electrical system alone, far more than the country could afford.

The effects of the sanctions have not been the same on all Iraqis. For a tiny handful of wealthy and/or high-placed individuals, war or no war and sanctions or no sanctions, life has remained comfortable. Saddam, the most privileged Iraqi of all, for example, is reported to have as many as a hundred personal palaces and mansions scattered around the country. These few fortunate individuals, who were able to divert a disproportionate amount of the nation's existing money and supplies to themselves, were little affected by the staggering 2,000 percent rise in food prices in the year or two following the war. But most Iraqis felt the full effects of shortages of food and hundreds of other diverse commodities. By 1996, inflation had become so severe that an Iraqi dinar (the country's main unit of currency), which had been worth $3.20 in 1990, was valued at just 1/2500 of a dollar. In Baghdad, new legions of the poor tried to sell their old clothes to make ends meet. And many people just gave up on money and went back

An Iraqi child holds up a photo of a starving infant, hoping to convince the U.N. to lift its sanctions against Iraq.

to the barter system, in some instances using chickens or eggs to pay the rent.

Not surprisingly, Iraqi children have suffered the most from the shortages created by the U.N. sanctions. In 1999, the U.N. estimated that as many as 20 percent of the country's children were malnourished. The year before, Denis Halliday suggested that "four thousand to five thousand children die unnecessarily every month due to the impact of sanctions because of the breakdown of water and sanitation, inadequate diet, and the bad internal health situation."[76] The suffering, psychological as well as physical, that lies ahead for these children can perhaps be predicted by looking at Iraqis presently in their twenties, who lived through the depredations of both the Iraq-Iran and Persian Gulf wars. A twenty-five-year-old Baghdad woman named Rana remarked to a Western journalist in 1999,

> We are a broken generation. My generation opened our eyes on war, the war with Iran. We all saw men coming home without an arm or a leg. We have only small dreams, and we are losing even those. Why does the embargo have to continue? Haven't we suffered enough?[77]

Saddam's Uncertain Future

Most Western leaders put the blame for these sad and deplorable conditions squarely on Saddam. They say that the sanctions remain in place mainly because he continues to refuse to meet the demands of the United Nations and Allies to reveal and destroy all of his weapons of mass destruction. When Saddam complies with his obligations regarding these weapons, they say, the sanctions will be lifted. By contrast, other authorities, including some international health workers and journalists who have actually visited war-ravaged Iraq, feel that most of the sanctions should be lifted immediately. In their view, the Iraqi people should not have to endure any further suffering, whether or not Saddam remains in power and defies the U.N.

Either way, most Western observers, as well as many people in the Middle East, agree that the dictator, Saddam Hussein, will eventually fall from power, most likely when his own people are finally fed up with him. Aptly summarizing this view, the Cockburns write,

> Any visitor to Iraq knows that . . . bitterness and hatred of their ruler . . . runs deep. Saddam's downfall will come at the hands of his own people, independent of outside intervention—a fact of which he himself is well aware. He knows that the rage and hatred of the masses, who for a few delirious days defaced his portraits and lynched his henchmen in [the rebellions in] March 1991, has not gone away. Sooner or later, there will be a reckoning.[78]

✯ Notes ✯

Introduction: A Short but Significant Conflict

1. Quoted in *Aviation Week and Space Technology,* "Persian Gulf Crisis Four Months Later," December 3, 1990, p. 22.
2. Quoted in M. Barone, "The End of the Vietnam Syndrome," *U.S. News & World Report,* August 20, 1990, p. 34.
3. Lawrence Freedman and Efraim Karsh, *The Gulf Conflict, 1990–1991: Diplomacy and War in the New World Order.* Princeton, NJ: Princeton University Press, 1993, pp. 430–31.

Chapter 1: Middle Eastern Sands Sow the Seeds of Crisis

4. Dilip Hiro, *Desert Shield to Desert Storm: The Second Gulf War.* New York: Routledge, 1992, p. 13.
5. Hiro, *Desert Shield to Desert Storm,* p. 14.
6. Max I. Dimont, *Jews, God, and History.* New York: New American Library, 1962, p. 400.
7. Quoted in Avigdor Haselkorn, *The Continuing Storm: Iraq, Poisonous Weapons, and Deterrence.* New Haven, CT: Yale University Press, 1999, p. 20.

Chapter 2: The Iraqi Invasion of Kuwait

8. Quoted in *Time,* "Iraq's Power Grab," August 13, 1990, p. 17.
9. Quoted in "Iraq's Power Grab," p. 19.
10. Quoted in *International Herald Tribune,* July 24, 1990.
11. Quoted in *New York Times,* August 3, 1990.
12. Quoted in Russell Watson, "Baghdad's Bully," *Newsweek,* August 13, 1990, p. 17.
13. Quoted in *New York Times,* August 3, 1990.
14. Quoted in *International Herald Tribune,* August 4, 1990.
15. Quoted in "Iraq's Power Grab," p. 22.

Chapter 3: "Desert Shield": The World Against Iraq

16. Quoted in Hiro, *Desert Shield to Desert Storm,* p. 527.
17. Quoted in *New York Times,* August 6, 1990.
18. Quoted in Thomas Friedman and Patrick Tyler, "From the First, U.S. Resolve to Fight," *New York Times,* March 3, 1991.
19. Quoted in Watson, "Baghdad's Bully," p. 18.
20. Quoted in *International Herald Tribune,* August 9, 1990.
21. Quoted in "Iraq's Power Grab," p. 22.
22. Quoted in *New York Times,* August 9, 1990.

23. Quoted in *New York Times,* August 11, 1990.
24. Quoted in Freedman and Karsh, *The Gulf Conflict,* p. 102.
25. Quoted in Freedman and Karsh, *The Gulf Conflict,* p. 102.
26. Quoted in T. Masland, "A Tide of Terrorism," *Newsweek,* February 18, 1991, p. 35.
27. Quoted in Masland, "A Tide of Terrorism," p. 35.
28. Quoted in Watson, "Baghdad's Bully," p. 20.
29. Quoted in *International Herald Tribune,* August 17, 1990.
30. Quoted in J. Bierman and B. Levin, "The Hostages in the Gulf," *Maclean's,* August 27, 1990, p. 25.
31. Jean E. Smith, *George Bush's War.* New York: Henry Holt, 1992, p. 134.
32. Quoted in *New York Times,* August 22, 1990.

Chapter 4: The Ominous Prelude to All-Out War

33. Quoted in Smith, *George Bush's War,* pp. 207–208.
34. Hiro, *Desert Shield to Desert Storm,* pp. 195–96.
35. Frank N. Schubert and Theresa L. Kraus, eds., *The Whirlwind War: The United States Army in Operations* Desert Shield *and* Desert Storm. Washington, DC: U.S. Army Center of Military History, 1995, pp. 210–11.
36. Quoted in *New York Times,* November 8, 1990.
37. Quoted in *International Herald Tribune,* November 29, 1990.
38. Quoted in Hiro, *Desert Shield to Desert Storm,* p. 261.
39. Quoted in "Persian Gulf Crisis Four Months Later," p. 23.
40. Quoted in Freedman and Karsh, *The Gulf Conflict,* p. 234.
41. Quoted in Freedman and Karsh, *The Gulf Conflict,* p. 235.
42. Quoted in *New York Times,* January 10, 1990.
43. Quoted in *Congressional Record,* 102nd Congress, vol. 137, Daily Edition, January 10, 1991, p. S101.
44. Quoted in *Congressional Record,* January 12, 1991, p. S377.
45. Quoted in *Congressional Record,* January 12, 1991, p. H169.
46. Quoted in Friedman and Tyler, "From the First, U.S. Resolve to Fight."

Chapter 5: "Desert Storm": The Massive Allied Air Assault

47. Quoted in *International Herald Tribune,* January 17, 1991.
48. Freedman and Karsh, *The Gulf Conflict,* p. 306.
49. Quoted in *International Herald Tribune,* January 17, 1991.
50. Quoted in *New York Times,* January 18, 1991.
51. Quoted in Hiro, *Desert Shield to Desert Storm,* p. 325.
52. Quoted in Hiro, *Desert Shield to Desert Storm,* p. 326.
53. Quoted in *International Herald Tribune,*

February 23, 1991.

54. Quoted in *International Herald Tribune,* January 24, 1991.

Chapter 6: The Lightning Allied Ground Offensive

55. Quoted in *International Herald Tribune,* February 24, 1991.
56. Quoted in Hiro, *Desert Shield to Desert Storm,* p. 387.
57. Quoted in Hiro, *Desert Shield to Desert Storm,* p. 387.
58. Quoted in Hiro, *Desert Shield to Desert Storm,* pp. 387–88.
59. Quoted in *International Herald Tribune,* February 28, 1991.
60. Quoted in *New York Times,* February 28, 1991.
61. Quoted in *New York Times,* February 28, 1991.
62. Quoted in *New York Times,* February 28, 1991.

Chapter 7: More Troubles for Iraq and the Middle East

63. Quoted in *New York Times,* March 7, 1991.
64. Quoted in Tom Morganthau, "The Military's New Image," *Newsweek,* March 11, 1991, p. 29.
65. Quoted in *International Herald Tribune,* March 4, 1991.
66. Quoted in Mike Edwards, "Eyewitness Iraq," *National Geographic,* November 1999, p. 22.
67. Quoted in *Maclean's,* "Why Saddam Won," September 16, 1996, p. 25.
68. Andrew Cockburn and Patrick Cockburn, *Out of the Ashes: The Resurrection of Saddam Hussein.* New York: HarperCollins, 1999, p. 244.
69. Quoted in "Why Saddam Won," pp. 24–25.
70. Edwards, "Eyewitness Iraq," pp. 25–26.
71. Cockburns, *Out of the Ashes,* p. 96.
72. Cockburns, *Out of the Ashes,* p. 97.
73. Quoted in Cockburns, *Out of the Ashes,* p. 43.
74. Quoted in Cockburns, *Out of the Ashes,* p. 43.
75. Quoted in Cockburns, *Out of the Ashes,* p. 135.
76. Quoted in Cockburns, *Out of the Ashes,* p. 285.
77. Quoted in Edwards, "Eyewitness Iraq," p. 20.
78. Cockburns, *Out of the Ashes,* p. 290.

☆ Chronology of Events ☆

1914–1918

The years of World War I, in which Britain and France organize many Middle Eastern Arabs to help them drive the Turks out of the region.

1917

The Balfour Declaration announces Britain's commitment to help the Jews find a homeland in the Middle East.

1922

The Anglo-Iraqi Treaty vests economic and military control of Iraq in British hands.

1932

The British end their mandate over Iraq, which becomes an independent country.

1945

The seven existing Middle Eastern Arab nations establish the Arab League.

1948

The Jews in Palestine proclaim the formation of the nation of Israel; Arab armies attack the fledgling country but are repulsed. (This will be the first of four Arab-Israeli wars, the others taking place in 1956, 1967, and 1973.)

1961

Kuwait, Iraq's tiny Arab neighbor, gains its independence.

1973

OPEC, the Arab oil cartel, imposes a major oil embargo on the United States and other Western nations.

1979

Saddam Hussein becomes dictator of Iraq.

1980–1988

The years of the Iraq-Iran War, a bloody conflict fought by Iraq and its non-Arabic neighbor, Iran, for control of the gulf region; the conflict ends in a stalemate.

1990

August 2: On Saddam's orders, Iraq invades Kuwait, igniting a major international crisis; in an emergency meeting called to deal with the situation, the United Nations demands that Iraq withdraw its forces.

August 6: The United Nations imposes a sweeping trade embargo against Iraq in an effort to persuade its government to vacate Kuwait; U.S. President George Bush orders troops to Saudi Arabia.

November 29: The United Nations adopts Resolution 678, authorizing military action against Iraq if it does not get out of Kuwait.

1991

January 9: U.S. and Iraqi representatives

meet in Geneva, Switzerland, attempting to resolve the crisis before January 15, the deadline set by the Allies for taking military action to liberate Kuwait; the talks fail.

January 16: The deadline having come and gone, the United States and its allies launch a massive air assault, dubbed "Desert Storm," on Iraq.

January 18: The world is stunned when Saddam retaliates by firing Scud missiles at Israel; at President Bush's request, the Israelis do not retaliate.

January 23: The Iraqis release huge amounts of oil into the gulf in an effort to damage a Saudi water facility; the result is an environmental disaster.

February 22: President Bush warns Saddam that he must remove his troops from Kuwait immediately or risk a ground assault by Allied troops.

February 23: The massive Allied ground attack, known as "Desert Saber," begins.

February 27: The Allies liberate Kuwait's capital, Kuwait City; meanwhile, the Americans and Iraqis clash in the largest tank battle fought since World War II.

March 3: Allied generals meet with Iraqi generals and negotiate a cease-fire.

March 6: President Bush addresses a joint session of the U.S. Congress and officially announces the liberation of Kuwait; many Iraqis, including the Kurds in northern Iraq, rebel against Saddam.

April–May: Saddam puts down the rebellions.

1996

Saddam attacks the Iraqi Kurds again; U.S. president Bill Clinton retaliates by ordering a cruise missile attack on Iraq.

1998

The U.S. attacks Iraq with cruise missiles again; in response, Saddam announces that he will no longer cooperate with U.N. inspectors who have been searching for evidence of his nuclear and biological weapons programs.

✯ For Further Reading ✯

Fred Bratman, *War in the Persian Gulf.* Brookfield, CT: Millbrook Press, 1991. A concise general synopsis of the war.

Warren Brown, *Colin Powell.* New York: Chelsea House, 1992. This biography of the top-ranking U.S. soldier during the Persian Gulf crisis and war is a commendable general portrait of a hard- working, self-made American military hero.

Christopher Chant, *The Gulf War.* New York: Marshall Cavendish, 1992. A general overview of the war, with numerous photos of soldiers, equipment, operations, and so on.

Paul J. Deegan, *Persian Gulf Nations.* Edina, MN: Abdo and Daughters, 1991. A fact-filled look at the various countries of the Middle East clustered around the gulf, most of whom took part in some way in the Persian Gulf conflict.

Leila M. Foster, *Iraq.* New York: Childrens Press, 1997. This provides some useful geographical, historical, and social information about the people of one of the leading participants in the Gulf War.

Zachary Kent, *The Persian Gulf War: "The Mother of All Battles."* Hillside, NJ: Enslow, 1994. A well-written overview of the conflict.

Bernard Lewis, *The Middle East: A Brief History of the Last 2,000 Years.* New York: Scribner's, 1995. An excellent synopsis of Middle Eastern history, providing valuable background information about the participants in the Gulf War. For advanced or ambitious younger readers.

✯ Works Consulted ✯

Books

Mary Louise Clifford, *The Land and People of the Arabian Peninsula.* New York: J. B. Lippincott, 1977. A useful general study of the Arabs of the region, who played an important role in the Persian Gulf War of 1991.

Andrew Cockburn and Patrick Cockburn, *Out of the Ashes: The Resurrection of Saddam Hussein.* New York: HarperCollins, 1999. A gripping, fascinating account of the prominent figures and events connected with Iraq and its continued strained relations with the West during the decade of the 1990s.

David C. Cooke, *Kuwait: Miracle in the Desert.* New York: Grosset and Dunlap, 1970. This book provides pertinent background material for understanding the principal participants in the Gulf War, in this case detailing how Kuwait came to be and its political position in the region.

Daniel C. Diller, ed., *The Middle East.* Washington, DC: *Congressional Quarterly,* 1990. A good, general summary and analysis of the region, its peoples, and its problems on the eve of the Gulf War.

Max I. Dimont, *Jews, God, and History.* New York: New American Library, 1962. This tremendously informative volume provides a sweeping, fascinating overview of the ethnic and religious backgrounds of the Jews and some of the other peoples of the Middle East, who eventually came to grips in the Persian Gulf War.

Trevor M. Dupuy et al., *How to Defeat Saddam Hussein: Scenarios and Strategies for the Gulf War.* New York: Warner Books, 1991. Contains a large number of facts and figures about the combatants in the Gulf War and speculates about Saddam's strengths, weaknesses, and abilities.

Editors of the Encyclopedia Britannica, *The Arabs: People and Power.* New York: Bantam Books, 1978. A useful overview of the Arab peoples of the Middle East on the eve of Saddam Hussein's rise to power in Iraq.

Lawrence Freedman and Efraim Karsh, *The Gulf Conflict, 1990–1991: Diplomacy and War in the New World Order.* Princeton, NJ: Princeton University Press, 1993. An excellent summary of the Persian Gulf War, with much detail about behind-the-scenes activities in the United States and Iraq.

Avigdor Haselkorn, *The Continuing Storm: Iraq, Poisonous Weapons, and Deterrence.* New Haven, CT: Yale University Press,

1999. A chilling overview of Saddam's programs for the development of weapons of mass destruction and the threat they still pose to stability in the Middle East.

Dilip Hiro, *Desert Shield to Desert Storm: The Second Gulf War.* New York: Routledge, 1992. This fine synopsis of the 1991 Persian Gulf War includes many direct quotes by the principal leaders and other participants.

Gary E. McCuen, *Iran-Iraq War.* Hudson, WI: G.E.M. Publications, 1987. An informative look at the bloody conflict often referred to as the "First" Gulf War.

Dan McKinnon, *Bullseye Iraq.* New York: Berkeley Books, 1987. The story of the Israeli raid that destroyed a significant portion of Saddam Hussein's secret nuclear bomb facility.

Judith Miller and Laurie Mylroie, *Saddam Hussein and the Crisis in the Gulf.* New York: New York Times Books, 1990. Written before the actual outbreak of fighting in January 1991, this work chronicles the main events following Saddam Hussein's seizure of Kuwait.

Jean P. Sasson, *The Rape of Kuwait: The True Story of Iraqi Atrocities Against a Civilian Population.* New York: Knightsbridge Publishing, 1991. A summary of the brutal treatment of Kuwaitis by Iraqis during the Iraqi occupation of Kuwait from August 1990 to February 1991.

Frank N. Schubert and Theresa L. Kraus, eds., *The Whirlwind War: The United States Army in Operations* Desert Shield *and* Desert Storm. Washington, DC: U.S. Army Center of Military History, 1995. This book contains much useful information about the U.S. Army, its personnel, and its equipment during the Gulf War.

Jean E. Smith, *George Bush's War.* New York: Henry Holt, 1992. The author chronicles the events of the months leading up to the war and is ultimately critical of some of Bush's tactics.

Bernard E. Trainor, *The Generals' War.* New York: Back Bay Books, 1995. An interesting discussion of the strategies employed by the generals on both sides in the Persian Gulf War.

Periodicals:

F. Ajami, "Hosing Down the Gulf's Arsonist," *U.S. News & World Report,* October 24, 1994.

R. W. Apple, "Devil of a War," *New York Times,* January 27, 1991.

R. Arias, "As War Claims Its First Female M.I.A., Melissa Rathbun-Nealy's Pals Recall One Tough, Spirited Kid," *People Weekly,* February 18, 1991.

Aviation Week and Space Technology, "Persian Gulf Crisis Four Months Later," December 3, 1990.

M. Barone, "The End of the Vietnam Syndrome," *U.S. News & World Report,* August 20, 1990.

M. Barone and D. Gergen, "The Building War Scenario," *U.S. News & World Report,* October 15, 1990.

John Barry and Evan Thomas, "A Textbook Victory," *Newsweek,* March 11, 1991.

John Barry and G. Vistica, "The Hunt for His Secret Weapons," *Newsweek,* December 1, 1997.

D. Berdnarz and V. Windfuhr, "Saddam's Survival in the Ruins," *World Press Review,* August 1999.

J. Bierman and B. Levin, "The Hostages in the Gulf," *Maclean's,* August 27, 1990.

Business Week, "The Gulf War," February 11, 1991.

B. Came, "Saddam's Secret Arsenal," *Maclean's,* November 24, 1997.

H. G. Chua-Eoan, "Strains on the Coalition," *Time,* December 10, 1990.

A. Cooperman, "Saddam Tells America: Get Out," *U.S. News & World Report,* November 10, 1997.

A. De Jasay, "Lessons from the Gulf War," *National Review,* May 27, 1991.

M. Dugan, "The Air War," *U.S. News & World Report,* February 11, 1991.

Mike Edwards, "Eyewitness Iraq," *National Geographic,* November 1999.

T. Fennel, "The High-Tech Battlefront," *Maclean's,* January 28, 1991.

M. S. Forbes, "Postwar Prosperity and Peace in the Middle East," *Forbes,* February 18, 1991.

Thomas Friedman and Patrick Tyler, "From the First, U.S. Resolve to Fight," *New York Times,* March 3, 1991.

Michael Gordon, "Outnumbered and Outgunned, Allied Forces Outfox Hussein," *New York Times,* February 28, 1991.

D. H. Hackworth, "Life with the Line Doggies: Saddam's Suicidal Assault on Kafji," *Newsweek,* February 11, 1991.

J. Howse, "An Uncertain Christmas," *Maclean's,* November 26, 1990.

J. D. Hull, "Fear and Loathing in Israel," *Time,* October 8, 1990.

J. B. Kelly, "America, the Gulf and the West," *National Review,* October 15, 1990.

M. Kramer, "The Cost of Removing Saddam," *Time,* October 24, 1994.

Charles Lane, "Arms for Sale," *Newsweek,* April 8, 1991.

J. Leo, "Protesting a Complex War," *U.S. News & World Report,* February 4, 1991.

L. Lief, "Rebuilding a Ruined Nation," *U.S. News & World Report,* March 11, 1991.

Maclean's, "Why Saddam Won," September 16, 1996.

R. Marshall, "'Don't Tread on Us': U.S. Missiles Slam Baghdad over a Plot to Kill Bush," *Maclean's,* July 5, 1993.

T. Masland, "A Tide of Terrorism," *Newsweek,* February 18, 1991.

Tom Morganthau, "The Military's New Image," *Newsweek,* March 11, 1991.

Tom Morganthau and Russell Watson, "Allied Blitzkreig," *Newsweek,* March 4, 1991.

J. D. Morrocco, "Gulf War Boosts Prospects for High Technology," *Aviation Week and Space Technology,* March 18, 1991.

National Review, "The New Face of War," February 25, 1991.

New York Times, "Excerpts from Schwartzkopf News Conference on Gulf War," February 28, 1991.

———, "Iraqis Surrender to Italian TV," February 28, 1991.

Newsweek, "Did Saddam Blink?" March 2, 1998.

E. Roulean, "America's Unyielding Policy Toward Iraq," *Foreign Affairs,* January/February 1995.

John Schwartz, "The Mind of a Missile," *Newsweek,* February 18, 1991.

K. R. Sheets, "Iraq's Environmental Warfare," *U.S. News & World Report,* February 4, 1991.

Evan Thomas and John Barry, "War's New Science," *Newsweek,* February 18, 1991.

Time, "Combat in the Sand," February 11, 1991.

———, "The Fog of War," February 4, 1991.

———, "Iraq's Power Grab," August 13, 1990.

U.S. News & World Report, "The Gulf War," February 18, 1991.

Russell Watson, "Baghdad's Bully," *Newsweek,* August 13, 1990.

———, "Desert Victory: After the Storm," *Newsweek,* March 11, 1991.

World Press Review, "Saddam Hussein Changes the Gulf Equation," September 1990.

———, "Saddam vs. the World," October 1990.

———, "Target: Baghdad," August 1993.

☆ Index ☆

✮ Picture Credits ✮

Cover photo: © Peter Turnley/Corbis
© Aero Graphics, Inc./Corbis, 39 (left)
© AFP/Corbis, 23 (top), 30 (left), 64 (left), 84, 94
AP/Wide World Photos, 31, 62, 67
Archive Photos, 64 (right)
© Bettmann/Corbis, 20, 24, 44, 49, 53
CNP/Archive Photos, 81
© Corbis, 7, 8, 18, 36, 39 (right), 48, 50, 63, 89
Department of Defense Still Media Record Center, 54, 71 (bottom)
© Owen Franken/Corbis, 34 (bottom)
© George Hall/Corbis, 32
© Hulton-Deutsch Collection/Corbis, 9, 11, 19
Imapress/Pascal Pugin/Archive Photos, 23 (bottom)
Copyright 1991, Los Angeles Times. Reprinted with permission, 52, 79
© Francoise de Mulder/Corbis, 15, 22, 27
Popperfoto/Archive Photos, 90
© Reuters Newmedia Inc./Corbis, 34 (top)
Reuters/Ceaser Assi/Archive Photos, 30 (right)
Reuters/Pat Benic/Archive Photos, 66
Reuters/Mark Cardwell/Archive Photos, 85, 87
Reuters/D.O.D./Greg Bos/Archive Photos, 60
Reuters/Richard Ellis/Archive Photos, 57, 61, 71 (top), 74, 82
Reuters/Jim Hollander/Archive Photos, 58
Reuters/Stephanie McGehee/Archive Photos, 28
Reuters/Win McNamee/Archive Photos, 42, 46, 56, 73
Reuters/Frederic Neema/Archive Photos, 83, 88
Reuters/Faith Saribas/Archive Photos, 83, 88

Reuters/Phillipe Wojazer/Archive Photos, 76
© Charles E. Rotkin/Corbis, 16
© David Rubinger/Corbis, 17
Arnold Sachs/CNP/Archive Photos, 47
Martha Schierholz, 10, 69
© Mark L. Stephenson/Corbis, 26
© Peter Turnley/Corbis, 5, 35, 37, 41, 75

✯ About the Author ✯

Historian Don Nardo has written many books for young adults about American history and government, including *The Mexican-American War, The War of 1812, The Declaration of Independence, The Bill of Rights, The Great Depression,* and biographies of Thomas Jefferson and Franklin D. Roosevelt. Mr. Nardo has also written several teleplays and screenplays, including work for Warner Brothers and ABC-Television. He lives with his wife Christine and dog Bud in Massachusetts.